VICTORY HALL PRESS

VICTORY HALL
YEARBOOK

DRAWING ROOMS I 180 GRAND ST, JERSEY CITY NJ 07302

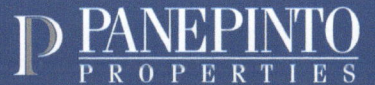

YEARBOOK PRODUCTION:
Interior Design/Layout: Alejandro Rubin
Editors: James Pustorino, Anne Trauben
Cover Design: James Pustorino

Victory Hall Press
180 Grand St.
Jersey City, NJ 07302
December 2017
ISBN-13: 978-1981326754
ISBN-10: 1981326758

This program is made possible in part by funds from the New Jersey State Council on the Arts/Department of State, a partner agency of the National Endowment for the Arts, administered by the Hudson County Office of Cultural and Heritage. Affairs, Thomas A. DeGise, County Executive, and the Board of Chosen Freeholders.

Table of Contents

Victory Hall Yearbook 2017 5

Drawing Rooms 6

The Big Small Show 7

Drawing Rooms 2017 Exhibits

    Bold and Beautiful 26

    The Innocence of Trees 30

    The Can–Man Show 34

    NJCU MFA Dress Rehearsal 38

    Sup-A-Genius: The Five Guy Show &

    Honoring Margaret: The Work of Margaret Weber 42

Rainbow Thursdays 46

Artists Work Spaces 48

Hand-In-Hand 49

The Art Project 50

Thanks 52

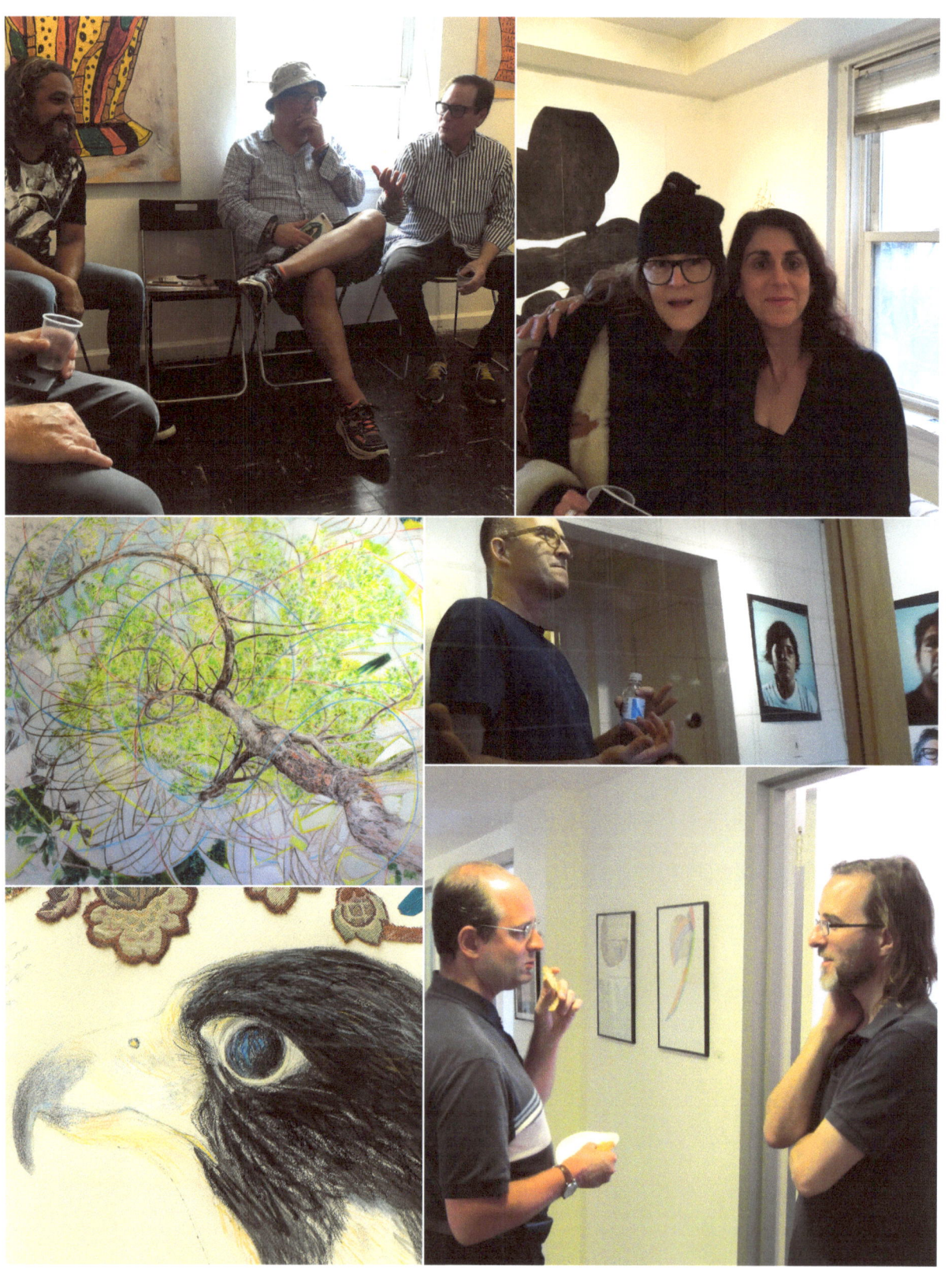

VICTORY HALL YEARBOOK 2017

Victory Hall Inc. was started as an organization in 2000 with the belief that the arts enliven, engage and sustain the hope of a community. This purpose was certainly on our minds all through this turbulent and politically urgent year.

In 2017 we produced Drawing Rooms' exhibitions that continued this mission and vision. We started the Spring with the courageous declarations of The Bold and the Beautiful, and are proud of the hope and strength of the works in this exhibit. This was followed by The Innocence of Trees, an investigation of nature and concerns for the environment. The Can-Man Show celebrated the artistic abilities of challenged men and women within our Rainbow Thursdays Artists program, and Summer's NJCU MFA Dress Rehearsal exhibition focused on new, developing ideas from talented young artists. In our two major exhibits for Fall, Honoring Margaret explored the vital imagery of a woman who was a founding artist of Drawing Rooms and a Jersey City arts pioneer, Margaret Weber, in over 30 works spanning decades, and Sup-A-Genius: The Five Guy Show, was a display of man-made art machines, from high tech to primitive tech that invited the public to witness or participate in the making of the work. Of course, the show of women geniuses will be on its way in the not too-distant future.

It's the fifth year of The Big Small Show, our small works exhibit that allows us to work with and bring together so many talented artists from across four states. Some of these artists are exhibiting in galleries locally and around the country, some exhibit internationally, and some are professors at universities. Some are curators, others are arts organizers who have developed their own art spaces. We are pleased to present their works to our community and are encouraged by their support of Drawing Rooms.

Rainbow Thursdays Artists, our program for developmentally disabled adults continued into its fifth year bringing weekly art classes to these amazing people, and their art was celebrated in three month-long public exhibits this year. Watching their growth as artists and the ever-changing ways they find to express their own sense of beauty and order convinces us again that art truly enriches one's life.

Our work in the community included producing over forty solo-artist lobby exhibits in newly designed Jersey City buildings as part of The Art Project, as well as ongoing shows of large-scale works at the expansive Gallery 109 Columbus space. We continued our activities with young people in the Hand-in Hand arts education program in Bayonne, creating mural and mosaic projects, and invited all ages to Drawing Rooms for group drawing days and artist talks and workshops.

Thanks to all the artists who work with us, and the public who visit our exhibits and engage in our programs, all the organizations we partner with and the Victory Hall Board of Trustees for joining us in making a difference in our community through art this year.

James Pustorino,
Executive Director

Anne Trauben,
Exhibitions Director / Curator

DRAWING ROOMS

Drawing Rooms is a contemporary art center in a former convent, featuring two and three-dimensional works by emerging and mid-career artists in NJ and the NY metropolitan Area. Located in vibrant downtown Jersey City, the gallery has 20 rooms, including the Tenth Floor Gallery Shop and Third Floor Artist Work Spaces.

Drawing Rooms is operated by Victory Hall Inc. a 501c3 non-profit organization producing exhibitions, programs and public art projects in the NJ/NY area since 2001.

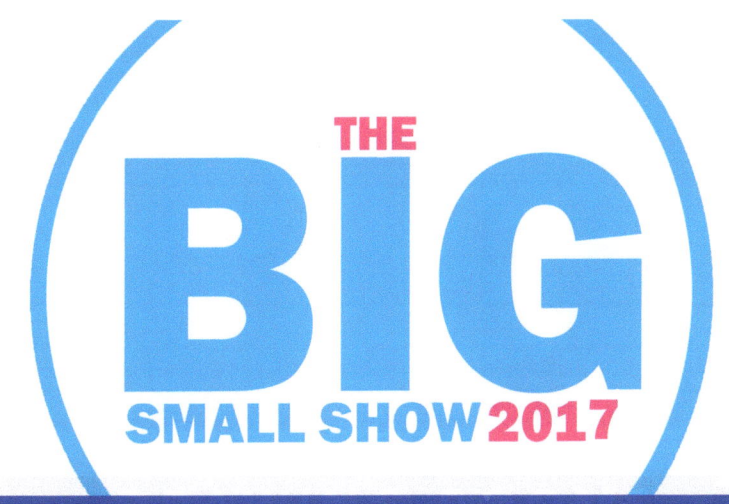

THE BIG SMALL SHOW 2017

DRAWING ROOMS

OPENING RECEPTION WEEKEND
Fri, December 15th (6-9P) / Sat, December 16th & Sun, December 17th (2-6P), 2017.

EXHIBITION DATES
Fri, January 12th to Sat, February 17th, 2018.

MEET THE ARTISTS (3-5P)
Sat, January 27th / Sat, February 3rd /
Sat, February 10th, 2018.

CLOSING PARTY (4-6P)
Sat, February 17th, 2018.

GALLERY HOURS
Friday 4:00pm to 7:00pm;
Saturday & Sunday 12:00pm to 6:00pm.

---

180 GRAND ST. JERSEY CITY NJ

Artists from all over New Jersey, as well as Brooklyn, Manhattan, and even as far as Connecticut and Pennsylvania, will be gathering for Jersey City's biggest small works exhibit of the year. THE BIG SMALL SHOW brings works by over 100 artists from across New Jersey and the NY metropolitan area together at Drawing Rooms. This survey of painting, drawing and three dimensional works completed in the last two years opens with a weekend-long reception beginning Friday, December 15th from 6 to 9pm and continuing on Saturday and Sunday, December 16th & 17th from 2 to 6pm.

THE BIG SMALL SHOW, in its fifth year at Drawing Rooms, features a large array of innovative and exceptional new works and allows visitors to discover artists new to them. The intimate setting of multiple rooms in this converted convent creates a place where art and artists connect with the public and with one another.

Curator Anne Trauben has met with artists throughout the year to select the participants and works: "For THE BIG SMALL SHOW we make full use of our multi-gallery room format to gather a selection of small works from each artist, grouping them in context together with one another, creating visual, formal and conceptual connections, amplifying themes and deepening ways of understanding the works. We are always including artists new to us in this exhibition along with artists who are part of our year-round community."

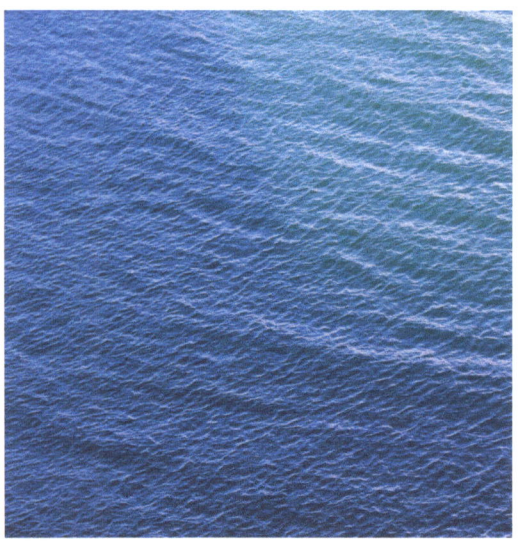

Fairborn
by Alejandro Rubin

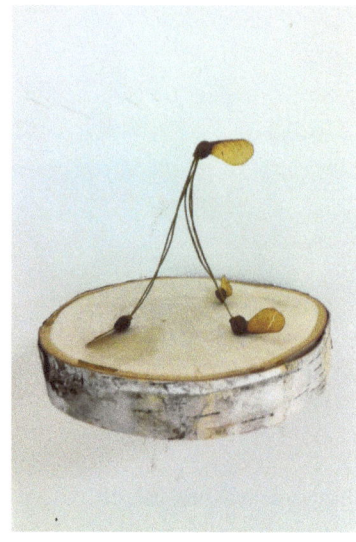

Clown
by Alice Momm

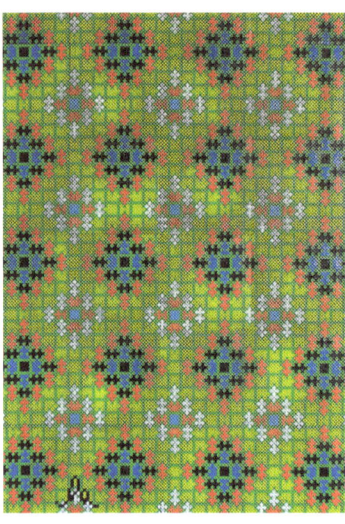

Dream Reflections
by Alpana Mittal

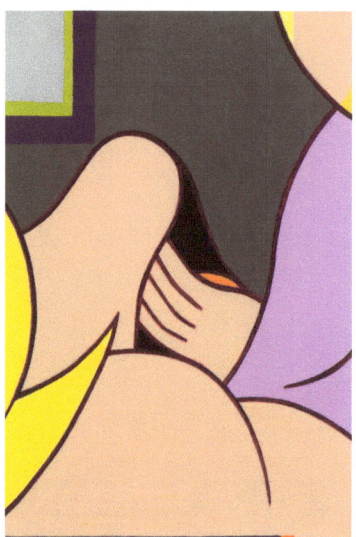

Self Portrait with Square
by Amanda Church

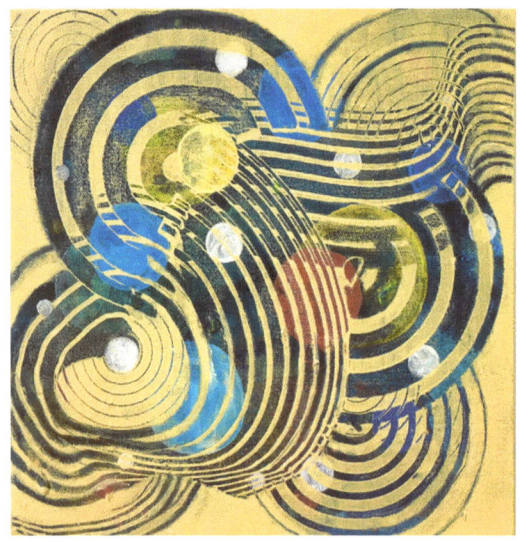

Small Worlds
by Andra Samelson

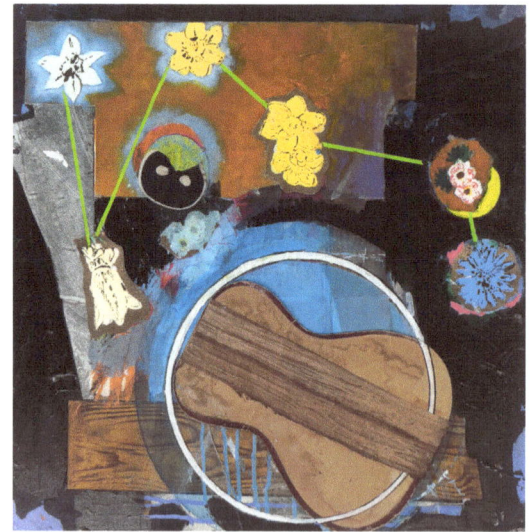

Spring Song
by Ani Rosskam

Fragments from the series In My Courtyard 0000 3831
by Ann Giordano

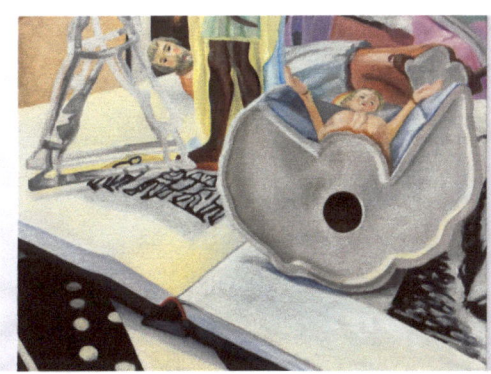

Tumble Four
by Anne McKeown

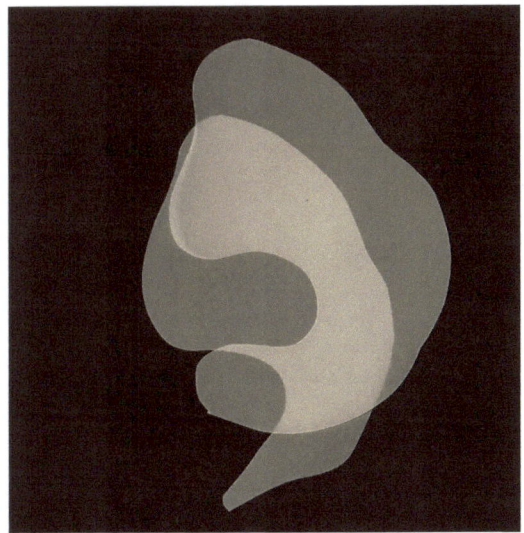

Untitled
by Anne Trauben

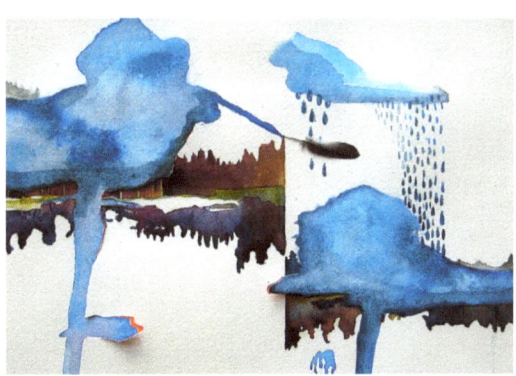

Feather Rain Divided
by Annie Varnot

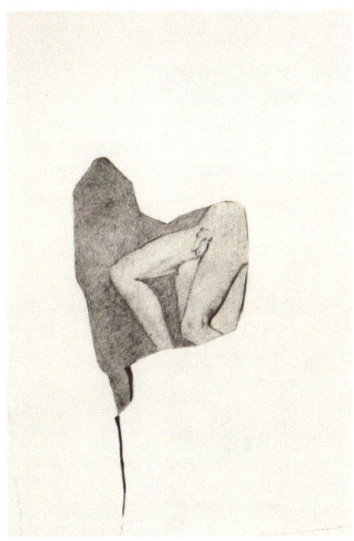

Cutout
by Ashley Lyon

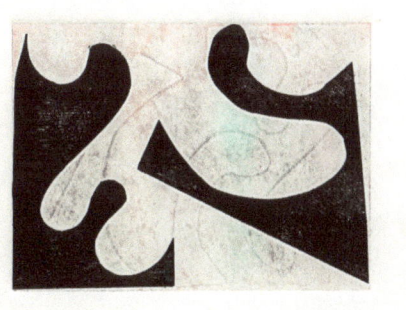

Kick 3
by Barbara Lubliner

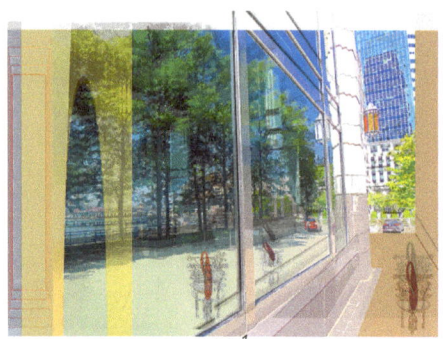

JC Waterfront Reflection 1
by Beatrice Mady

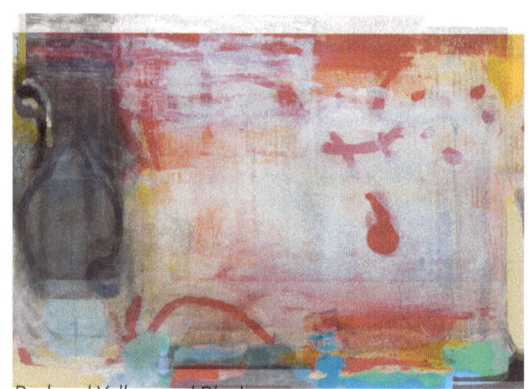

Red and Yellow and Black
by Bill leech

2-Part Invention
by Bill Rybak

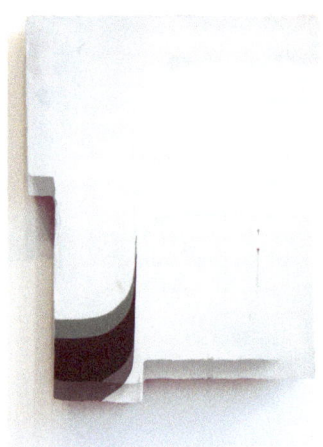

Diver
by Bruce Halpin

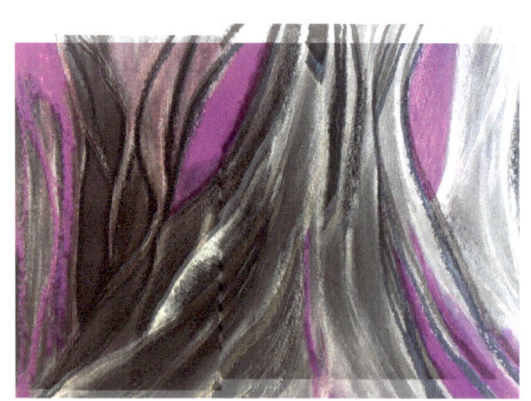

Roots
by Caridad Kennedy

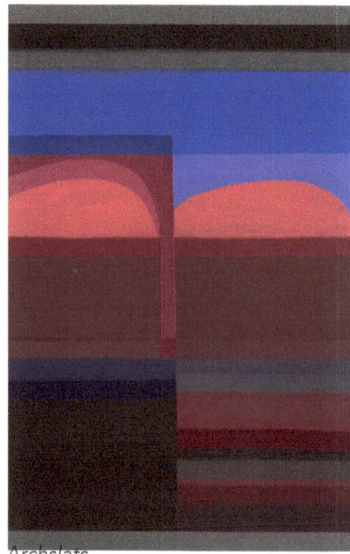

Archslats
by Carla Aurich

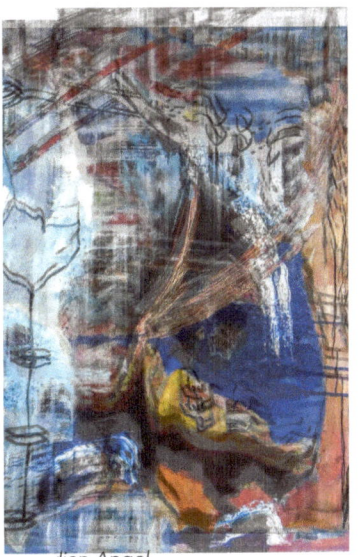

Guardian Angel
by Cathy Diamond

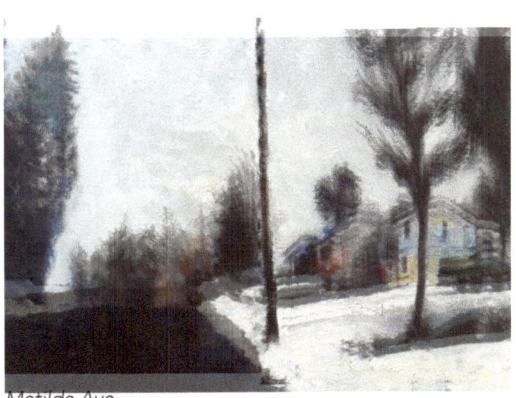

Matilda Ave
by Christopher Johnson

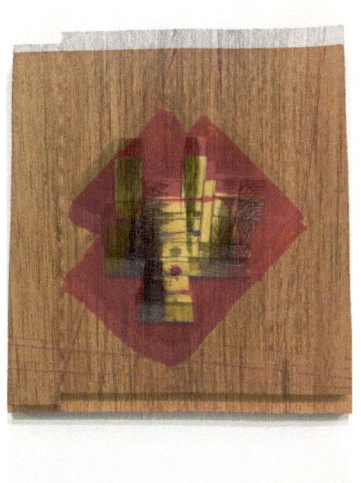

Unseen Violations
by Curt Ikens

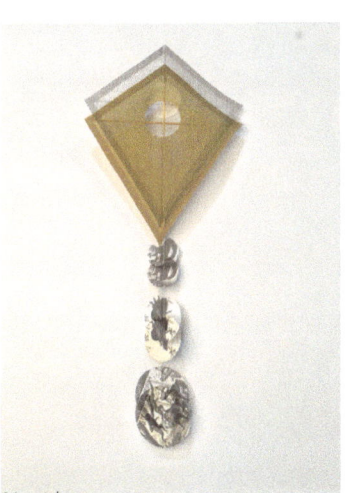

No title
by Dana Kane

untitled 4
by David French

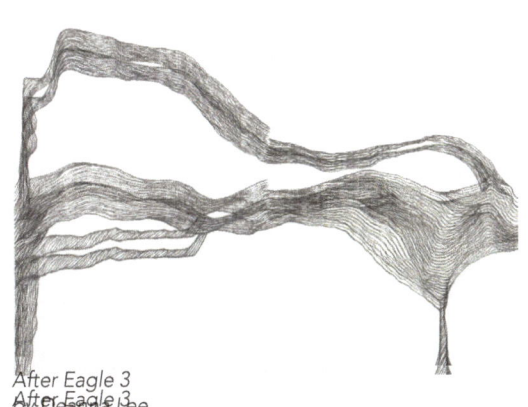

After Eagle 3
by Deanna Lee

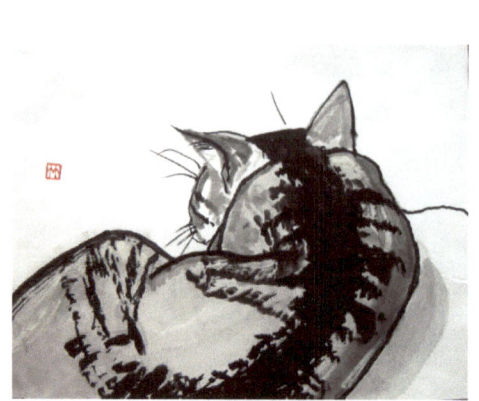
Senseiscat 7
by Deirdre Kennedy

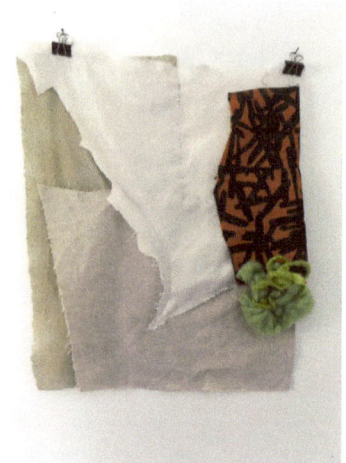
Brainfruit
by Diane Tenerelli-June

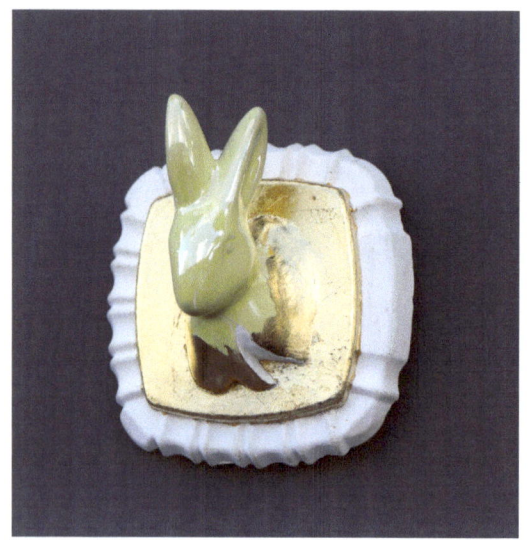
Rabbit Trophy
by Donna Conklin King

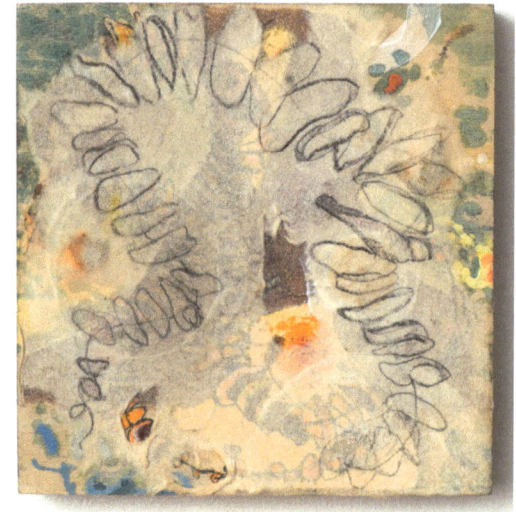
Whelk egg casings
by Eileen Ferara

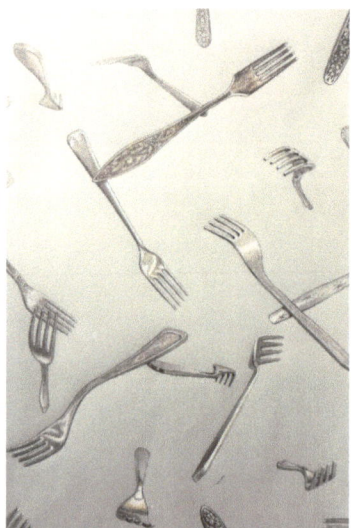
I Don't Give A Flying Fork
by Fran Beallor

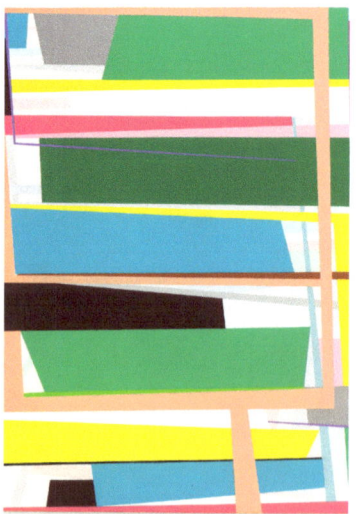
Don t Mind Me
by Gary Petersen

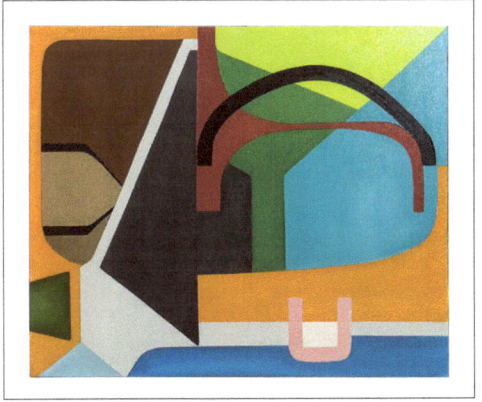

Number Thirty
by Greg Letson

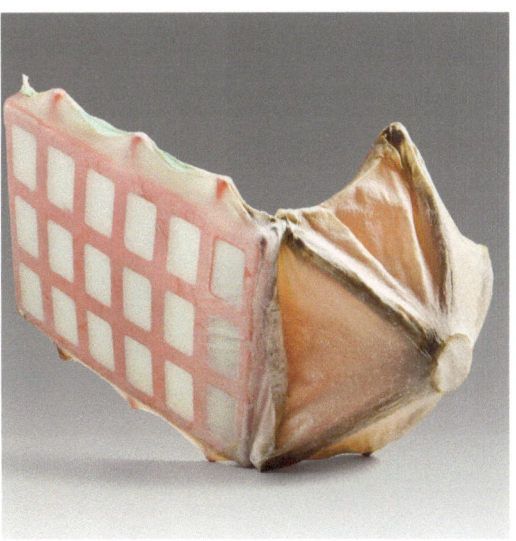

A.M. #7
by Ilene Sunshine

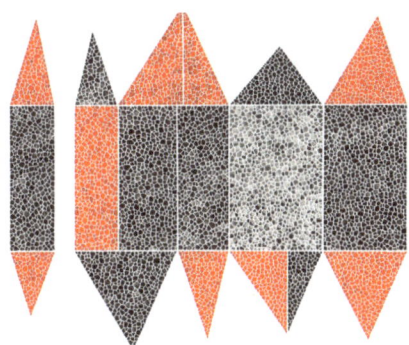

Untitled 01
by Injoo Whang

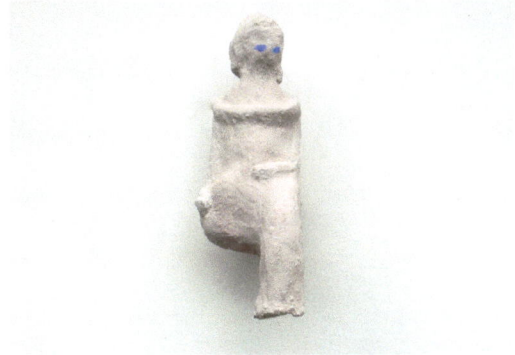

A Lost Lady
by Jackie Shatz

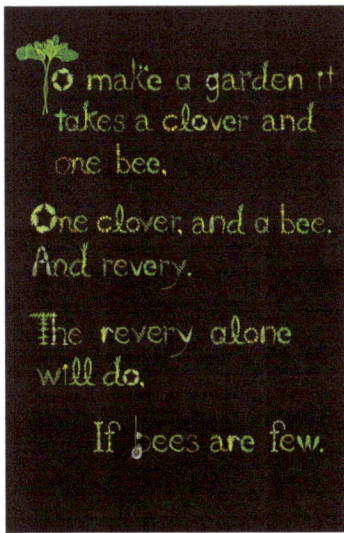

Bee Poem
by Janet Pihlblad

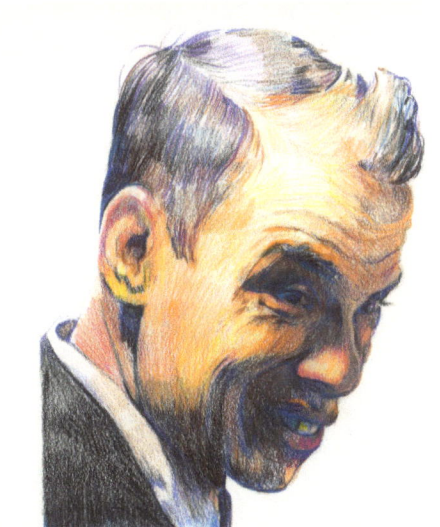

Wayne "The Train" Hancock
by Janet Tsakis

Mottainai 13
by Jeanne Heifetz

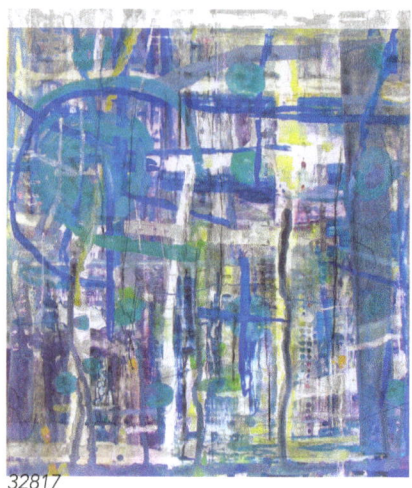

32817
by Jeanne Tremel

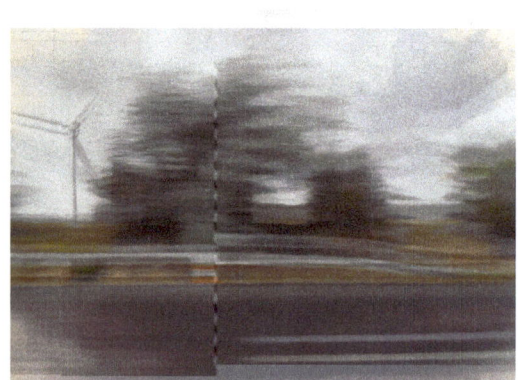

Eolienne II
by Jennifer Krause Chapeau

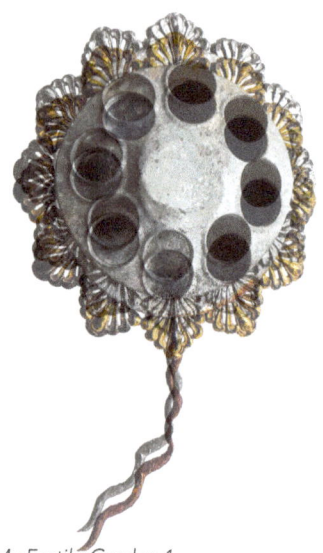

My Fertile Garden 1
by Jodie Fink

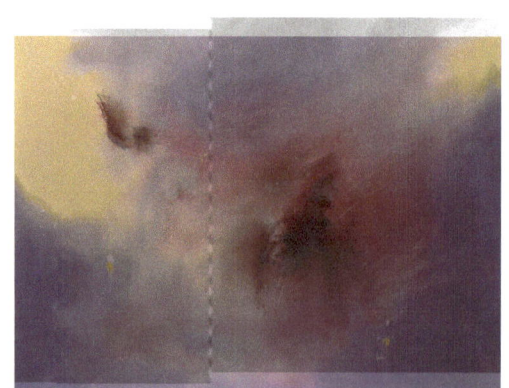

Dire Day
by Joe Lugara

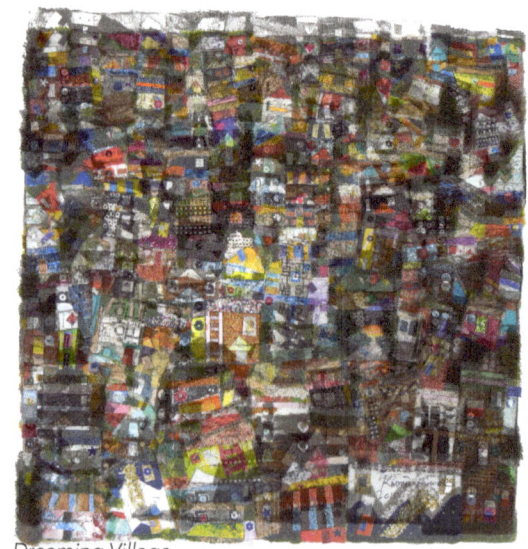

Dreaming Village
by Jong Hyun Kwon

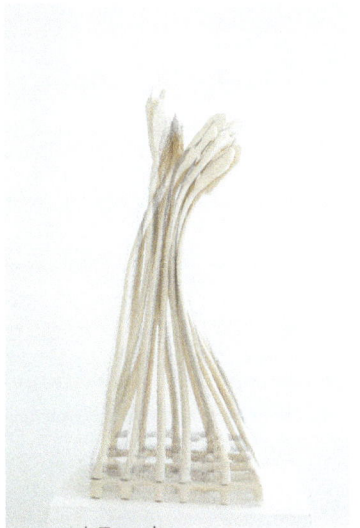

Lets Stick Together
by Josef Zutelgte

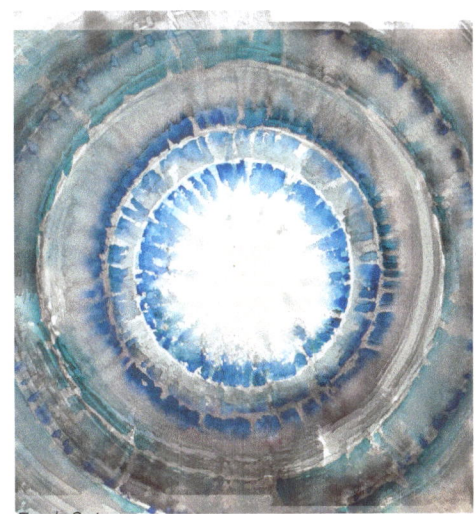

Earth Spin
by Julian Jackson

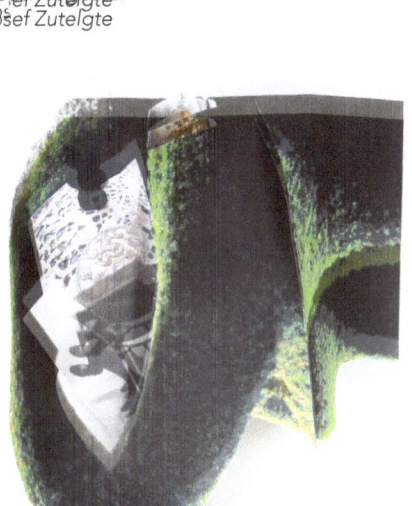

Chair Hedge
by Justin Pollmann

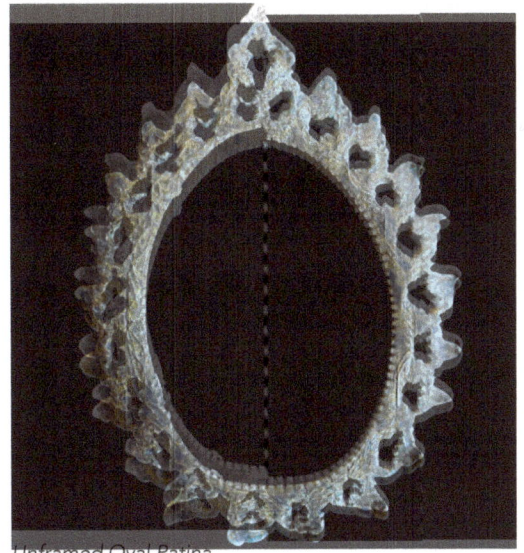

Unframed Oval Patina
by Katarina Wong

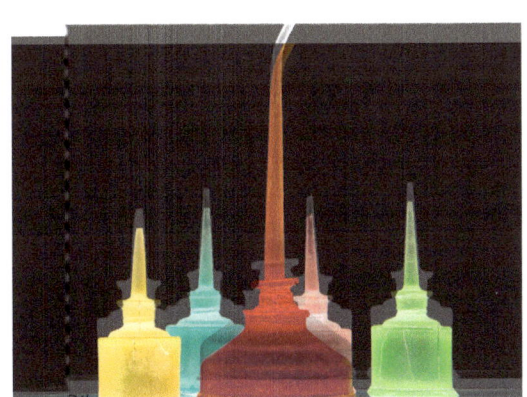

Little Oil
by Katherine Jackson

I Lost It Here IV
by Katherine Parker

The Big Small Show

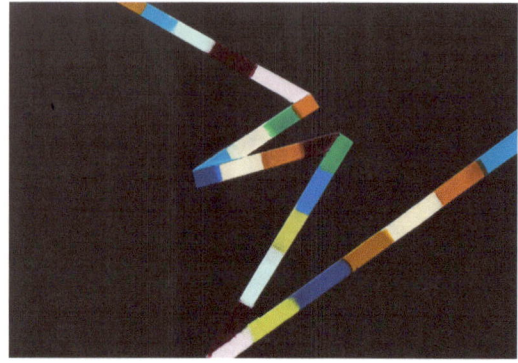

Walking Line 10
by Kathy Cantwell

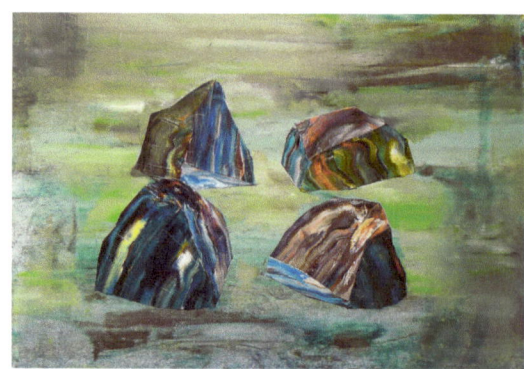

Rocky Quorum
by Katrina Bello

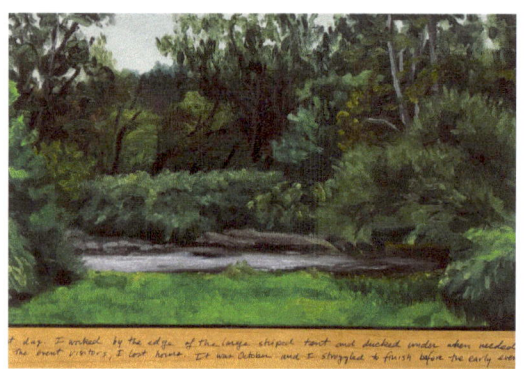

Callicoon Creek Park
by Kit Sailer

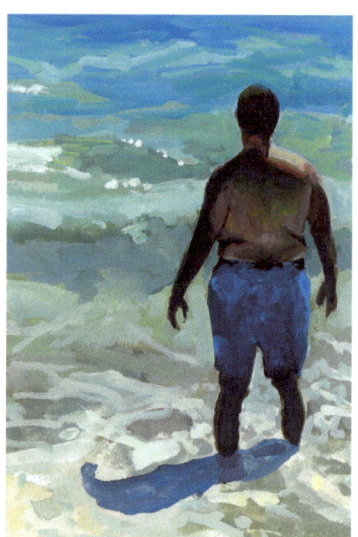

Big Man of the Beach
by Laura Alexander

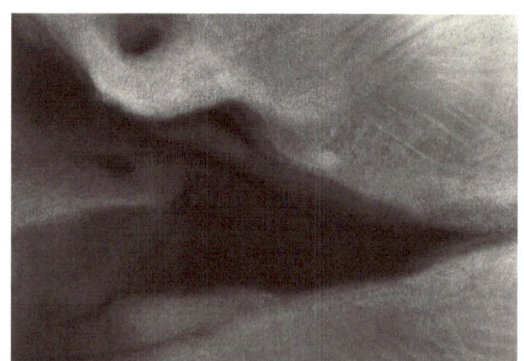

Red River Gorge Series
by Laura Lou Levy

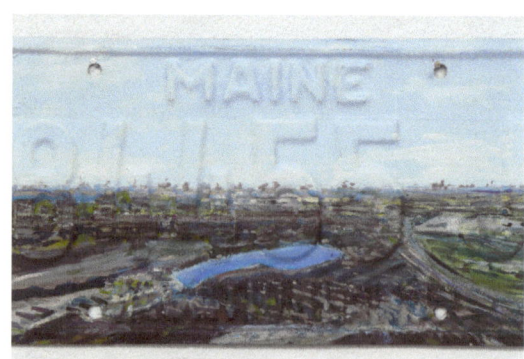

New Jersey Series (Dwasline)
by Linda Gottesfeld

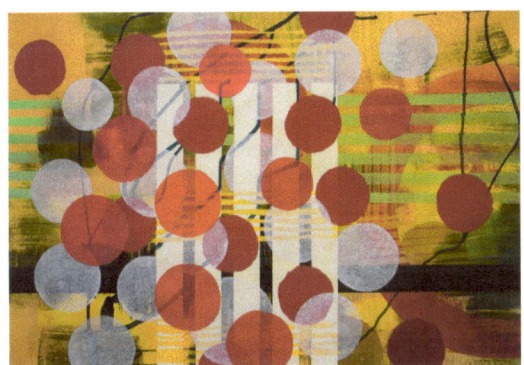

Mass
by Linda Schmidt

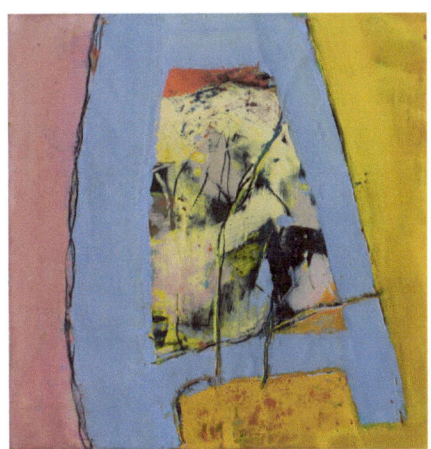

Decipher 16
by Lisa Pressman

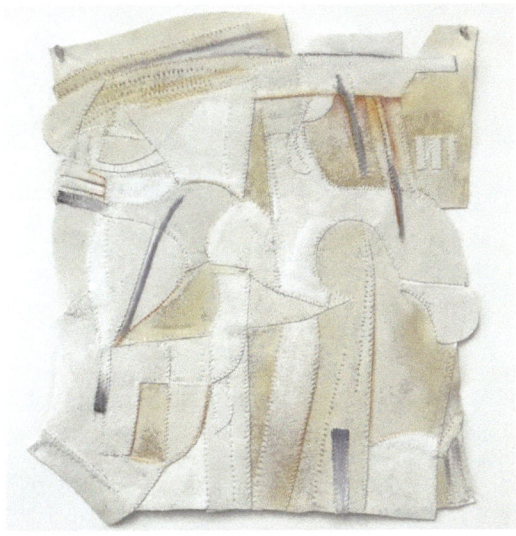

Hope is the Thing
by Lisa Sanders

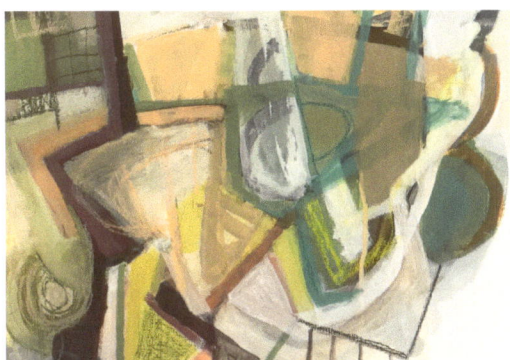

Hold The Mail
by Liz Atlas

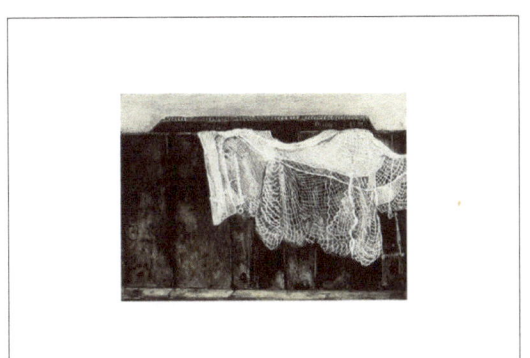

Fishing Nets on Wall
by Loura van der Meule

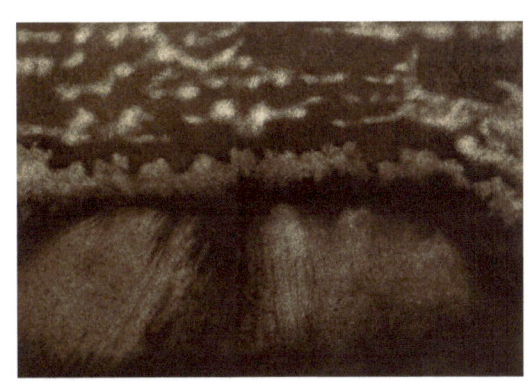

Soft and Sere
by Lucy Meskill

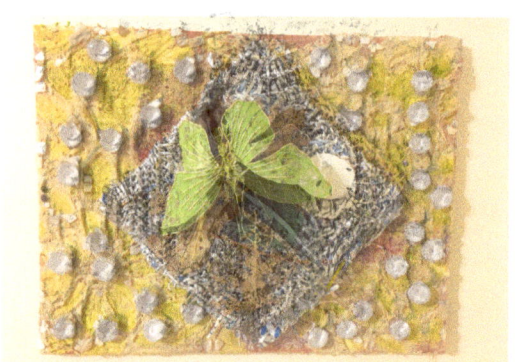
Celine
by Maggie Ens

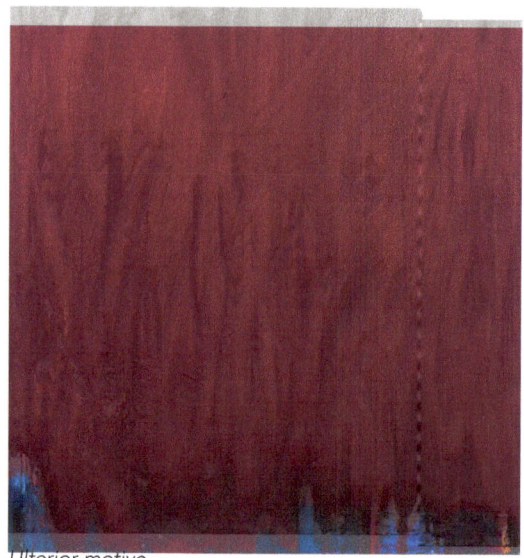
Ulterior-motive
by Marianne DeAngelis

Quartet 4
by Marietta Hoferer

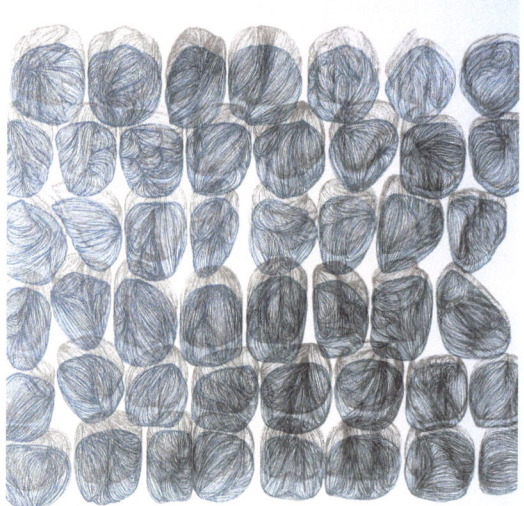
Untitled 01
by Mary Valverde

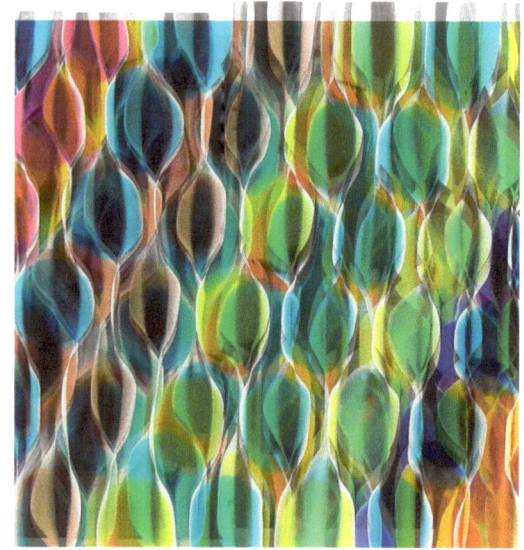
Untitled (DS-BR7)
by Maureen McQuillan

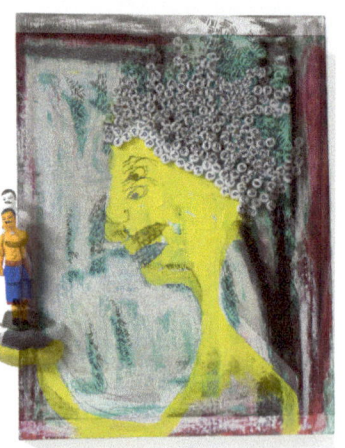
New Boyfriend
by Melissa Stern

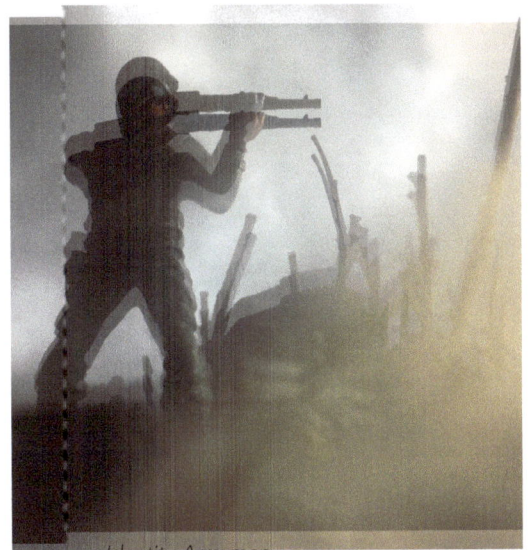

American Identity-Armyman
by Michael Endy

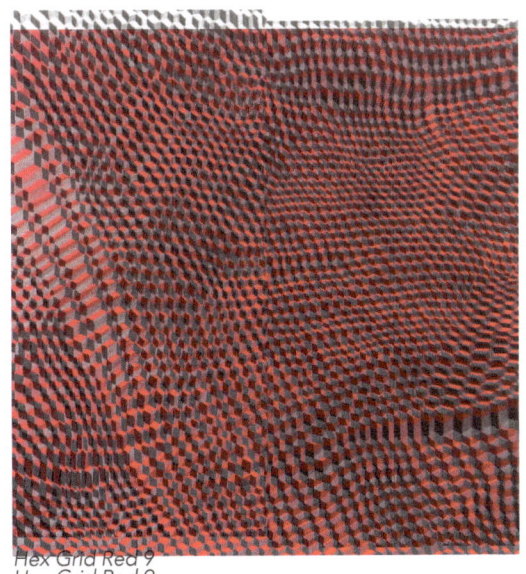

Hex Grid Red 9
by Michael Kukla

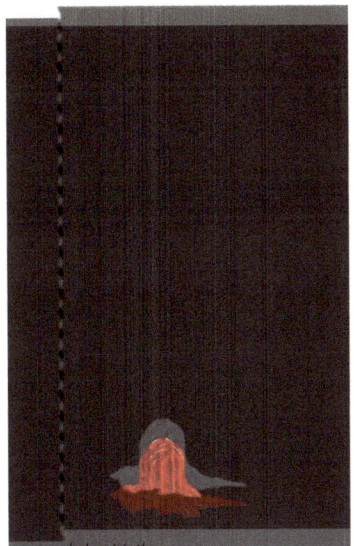

Behind the Veil
by Michael Moore

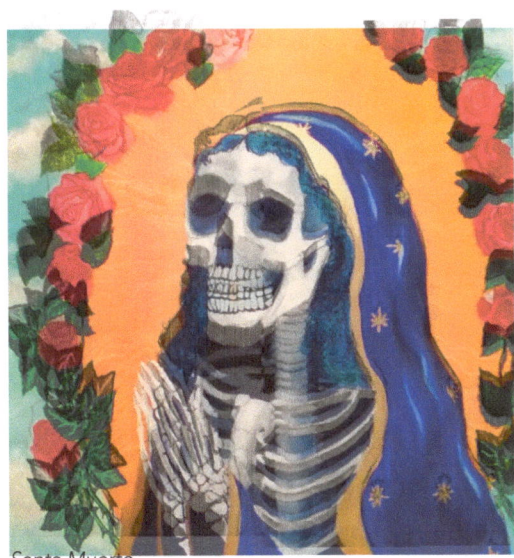

Santa Muerte
by Michael Teters

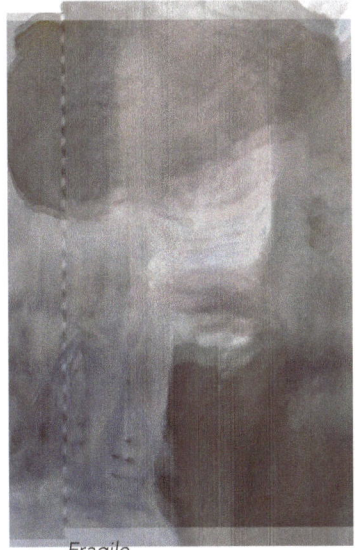

While Fragile
by Mona Brody

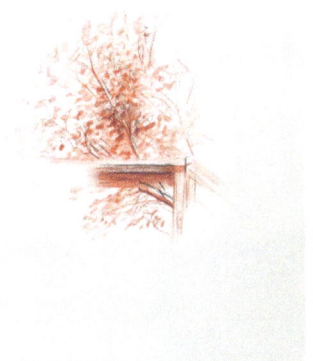

What the Bird Has Forgotten
by Nan Ring

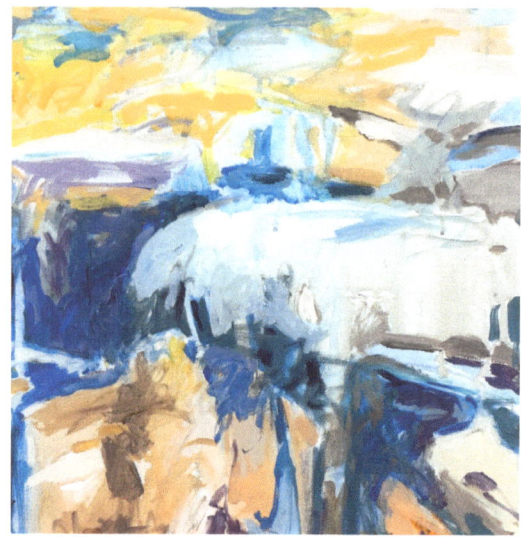

Cold Sun
by Nancy Karpf

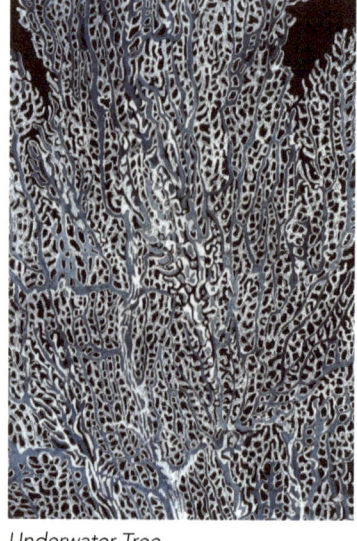

Underwater Tree
by Nikolina Kovalenko

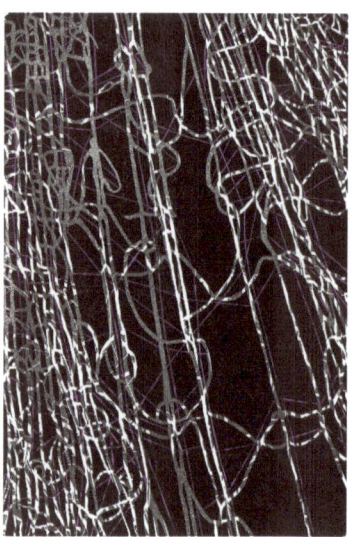

Ghost Nets
by Noémie Jennifer

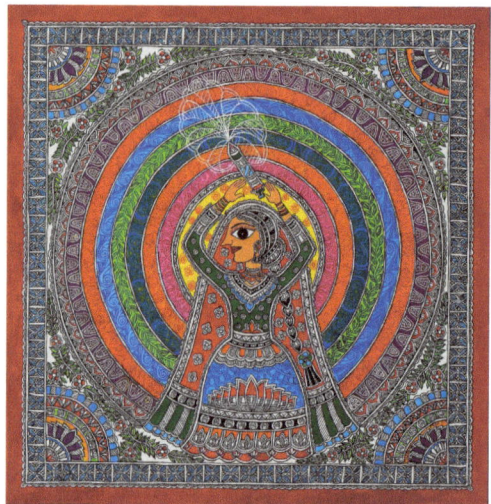

Rangotsav (Celebration Of Colors)
by Nupur Nishith

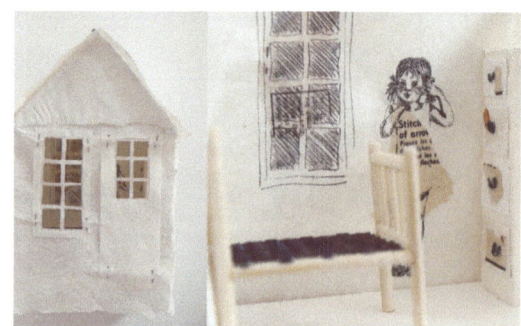

My-space XI
by Pam Cooper

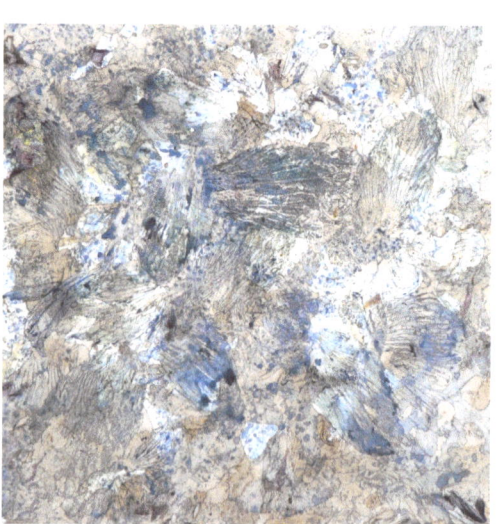

Data Drawing #33
by Pamela Shipley

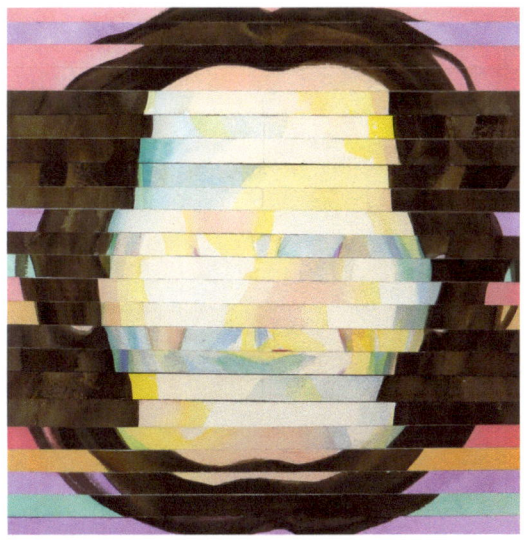

No Face
by Patricia Fabricant

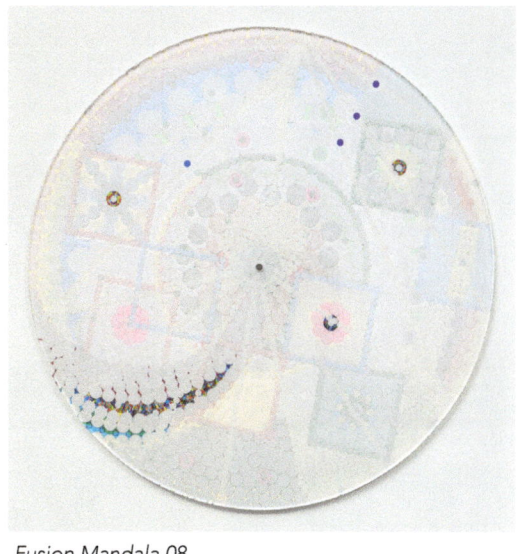

Fusion Mandala 08
by Pauline Galiana

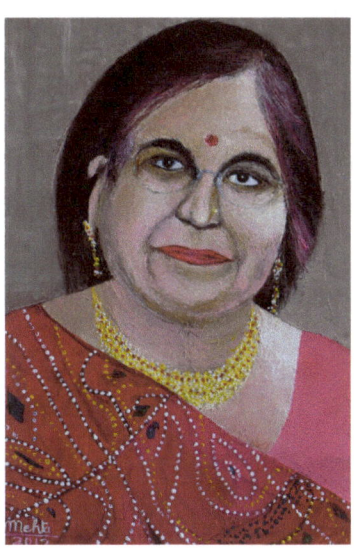

RAJ
by Rajendra Mehta

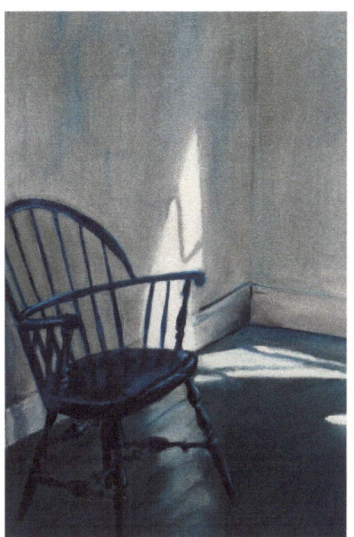

A Presence Light 1
by Rene Lynch

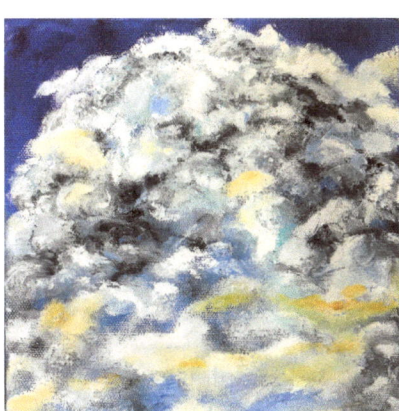

Thunder Cloud
by Rita Marie Cimini

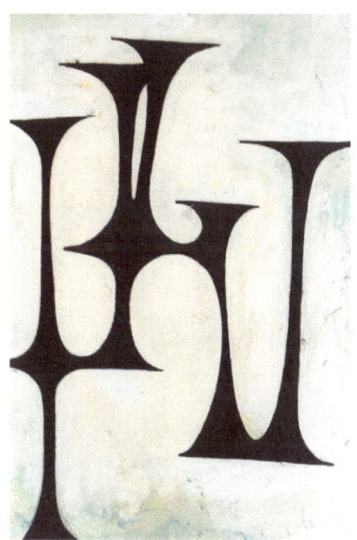

Denuntiatio
by Robert Egert

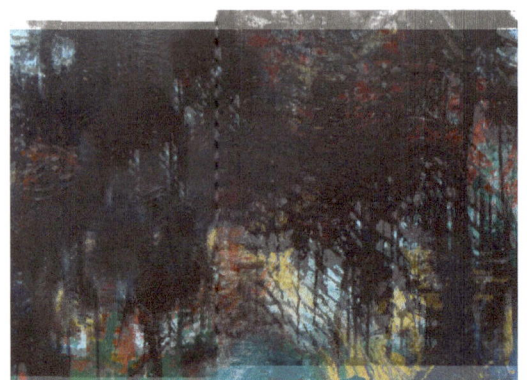

Dark Web
by Robin Feld

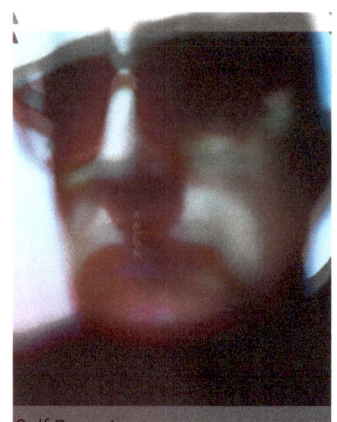

Self Portrait
by Roger Sayre

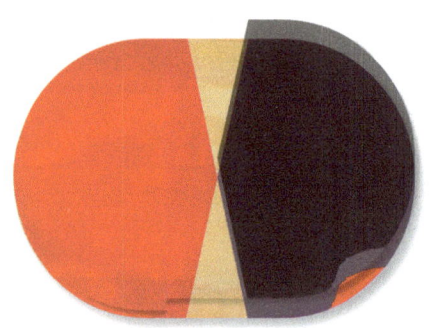

Duplicate
by Ruth Hiller

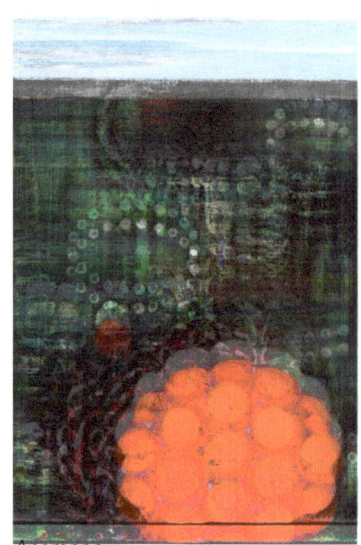

Anemone
by Sarah Lutz

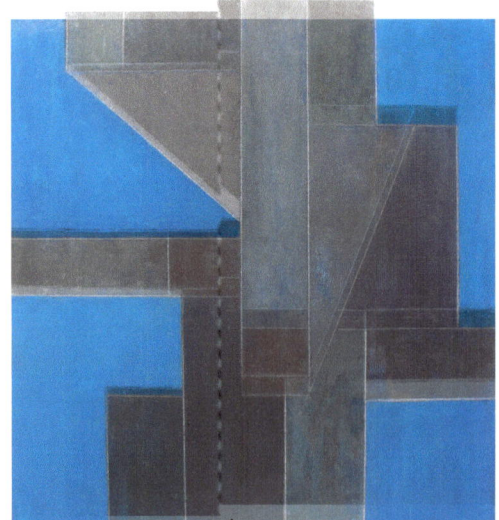

Pictures Of Something 4
by Stephen Cimini

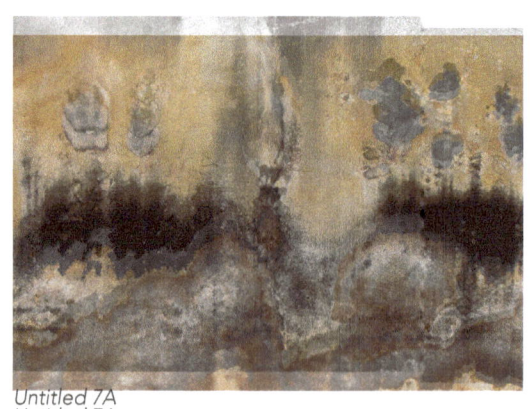

Untitled 7A
by Stephen Krasner

22   The Big Small Show

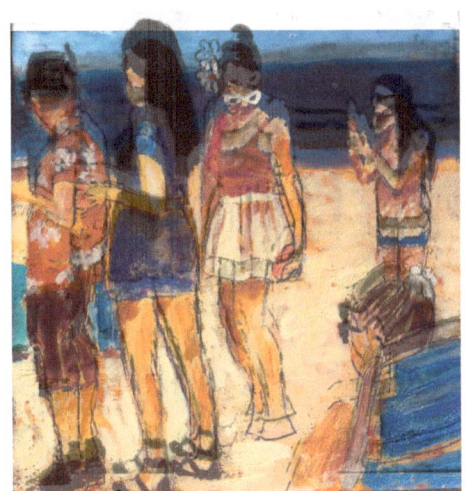

Asbury Surf Plot Twist
by Sue Ellen Leys

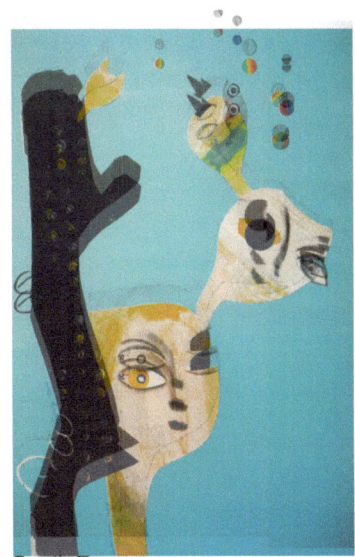

Family Tree
by Sunjin Lee

At the Still Point 31
by Tamar Zinn

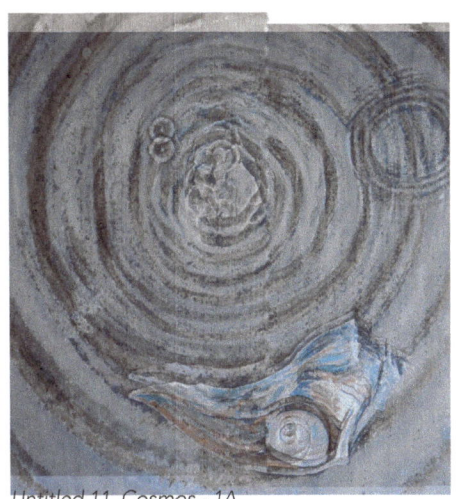

Untitled 11, Cosmos - 1A
by Terri Amig

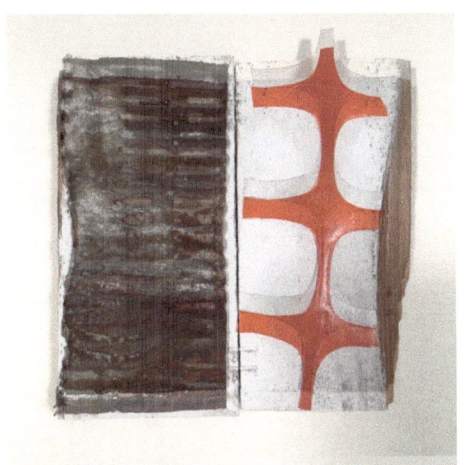

Brooklyn Navy Yards
by Tessa Grundon

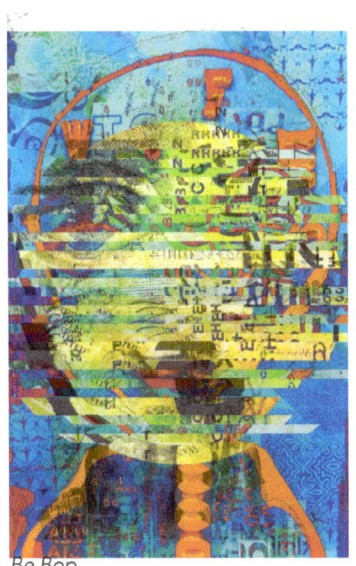

Be Bop
by Theda Sandiford

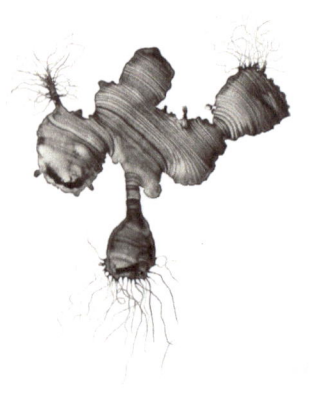

Grounding 1
by Todd Lambrix

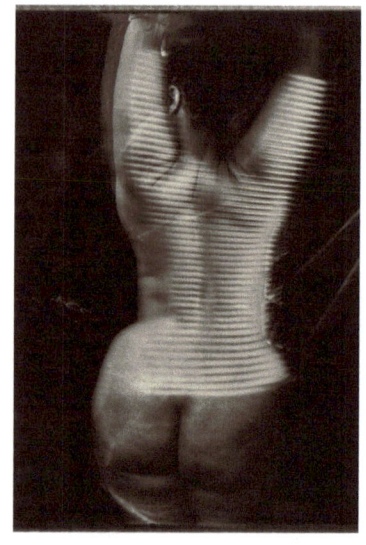

Corset of Light
by Trix Rosen

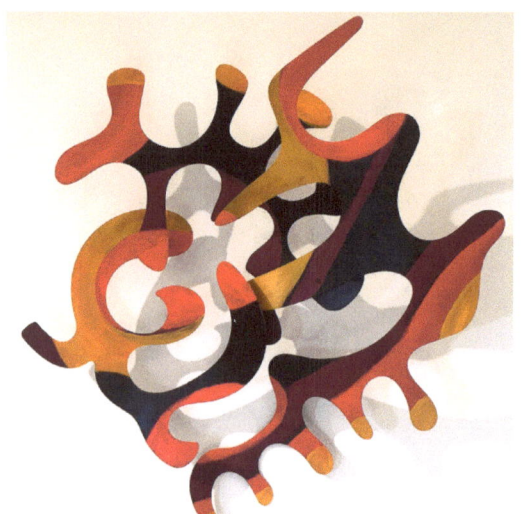

Ligature
by Wendy Letven

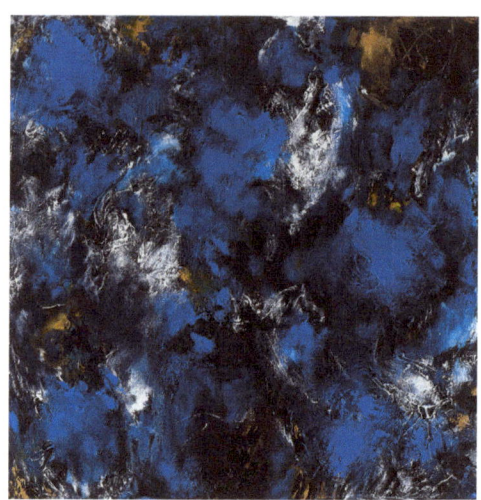

Galapagos Memory 4
by Yael Dresdner

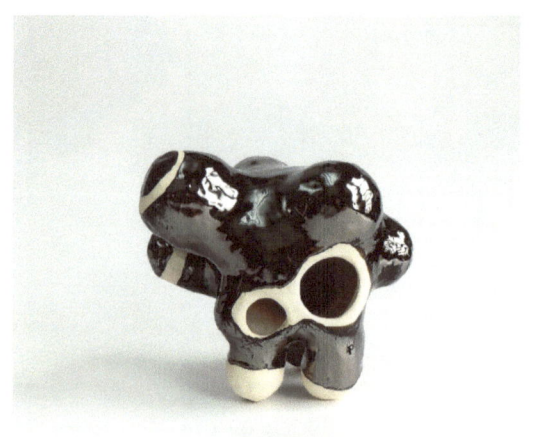

The Largest Crop 1
by Yuko-Nishikawa

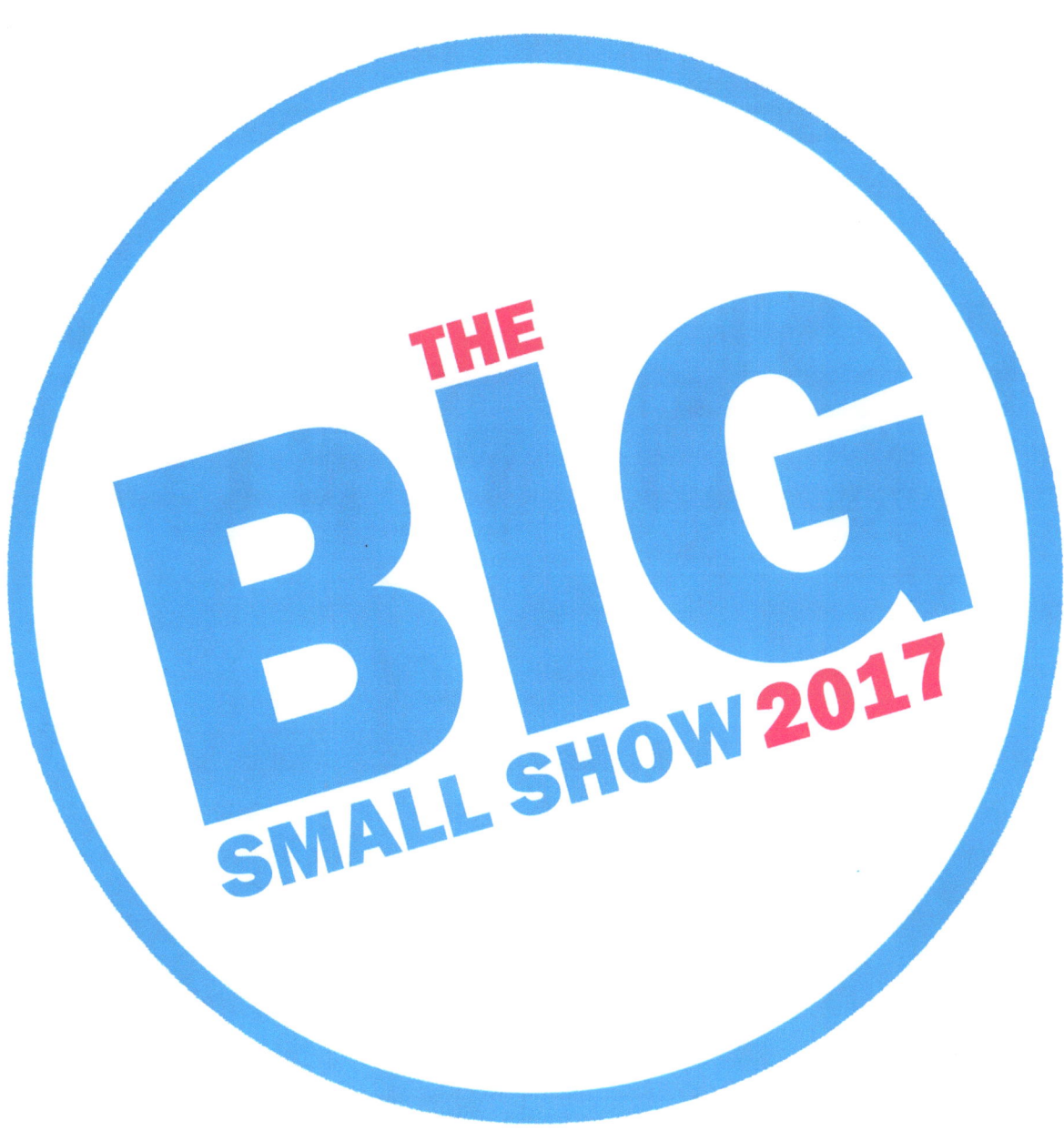

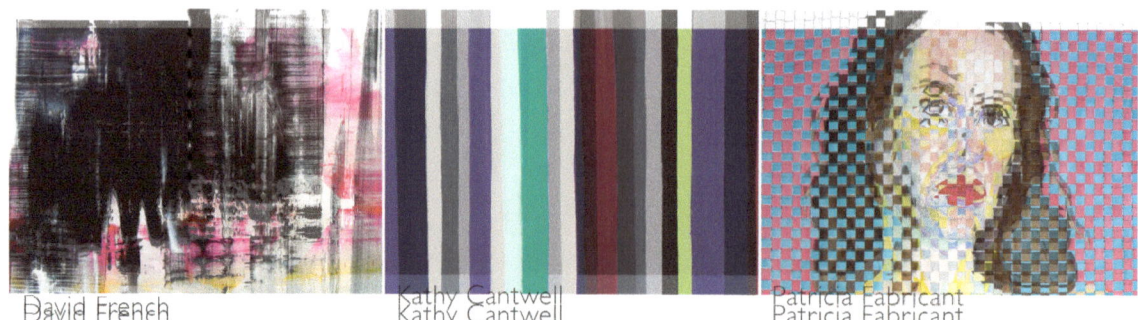

BOLD AND BEAUTIFUL

Curated by Anne Trauben

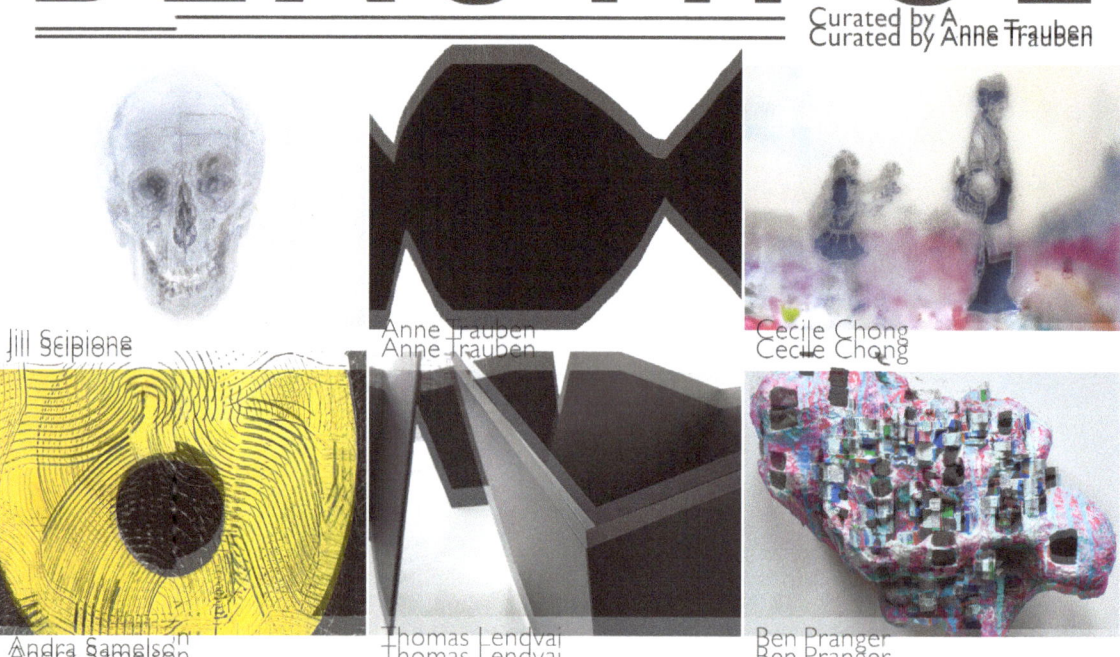

EXHIBITION: Friday 3/10/17 – Saturday 4/8/17
RECEPTION: Sunday, 3/12/17, 3:00pm – 6:00pm
WORKSHOP/TALK: 3/25, 3/26, 3:00pm – 6:00pm

Bold and Beautiful is an exhibit featuring drawing, painting, sculpture and installation by Andra Samelson, Anne Trauben, Ben Pranger, Cecile Chong, David French, Jill Scibione, Kathy Cantwell, Patricia Fabricant and Thomas Lendvai, each artist in their own gallery room, who come together to be bold and beautiful in their work, ideas and outlook. The exhibition is curated by Anne Trauben.

Bold and Beautiful is our initial 2017 response to the current challenges we face in this country. According to Curator Anne Trauben, "in this political climate we need to be bold and replenish ourselves by looking at beautiful things". Andra Samelson creates swirling ornate forms with incised lines that refer to microcosmic and macrocosmic occurrences. Anne Trauben explores form in large dark oil pastel drawings,

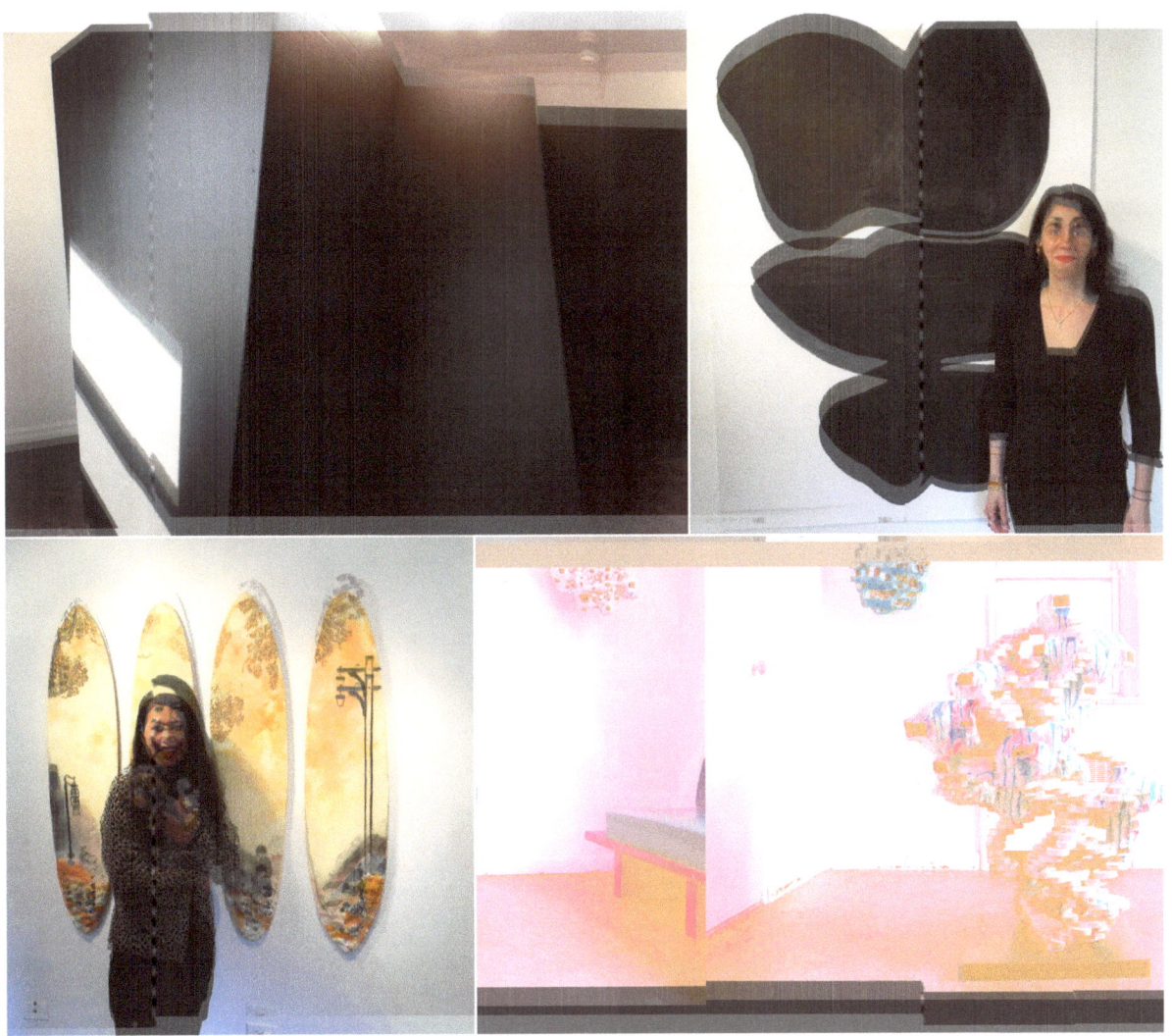

white wire and black and white ceramics. **Ben Pranger** makes precarious sculptures of complex sci-fi systems in paper-mache' and wood. **Cecile Chong** blends her Chinese and Ecuadorian cultures in complex images made of 25 layers of encaustic wax. **David French's** massive metallic paintings of silver light and black darkness refer to his personal experience with platinum-based chemotherapy. **Jill Scipione** creates stark, pencil skull portraits of females and developmentally disabled people from historic sources. **Kathy Cantwell** surrounds the viewer with her "Secret Life of Stripes". **Patricia Fabricant** presents confrontational self portraits. **Thomas Lendvai** changes the orientation of the space itself with his site-situated construction.

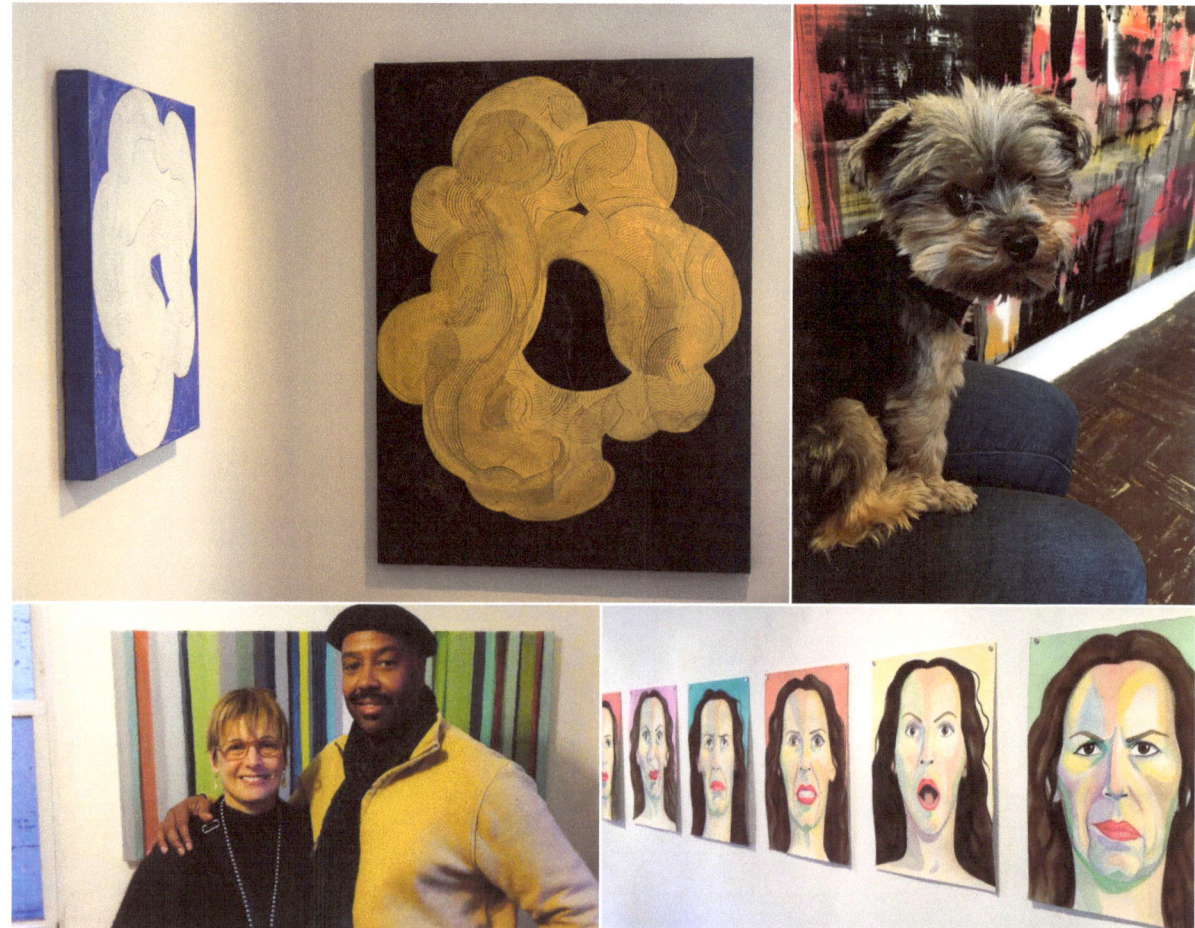

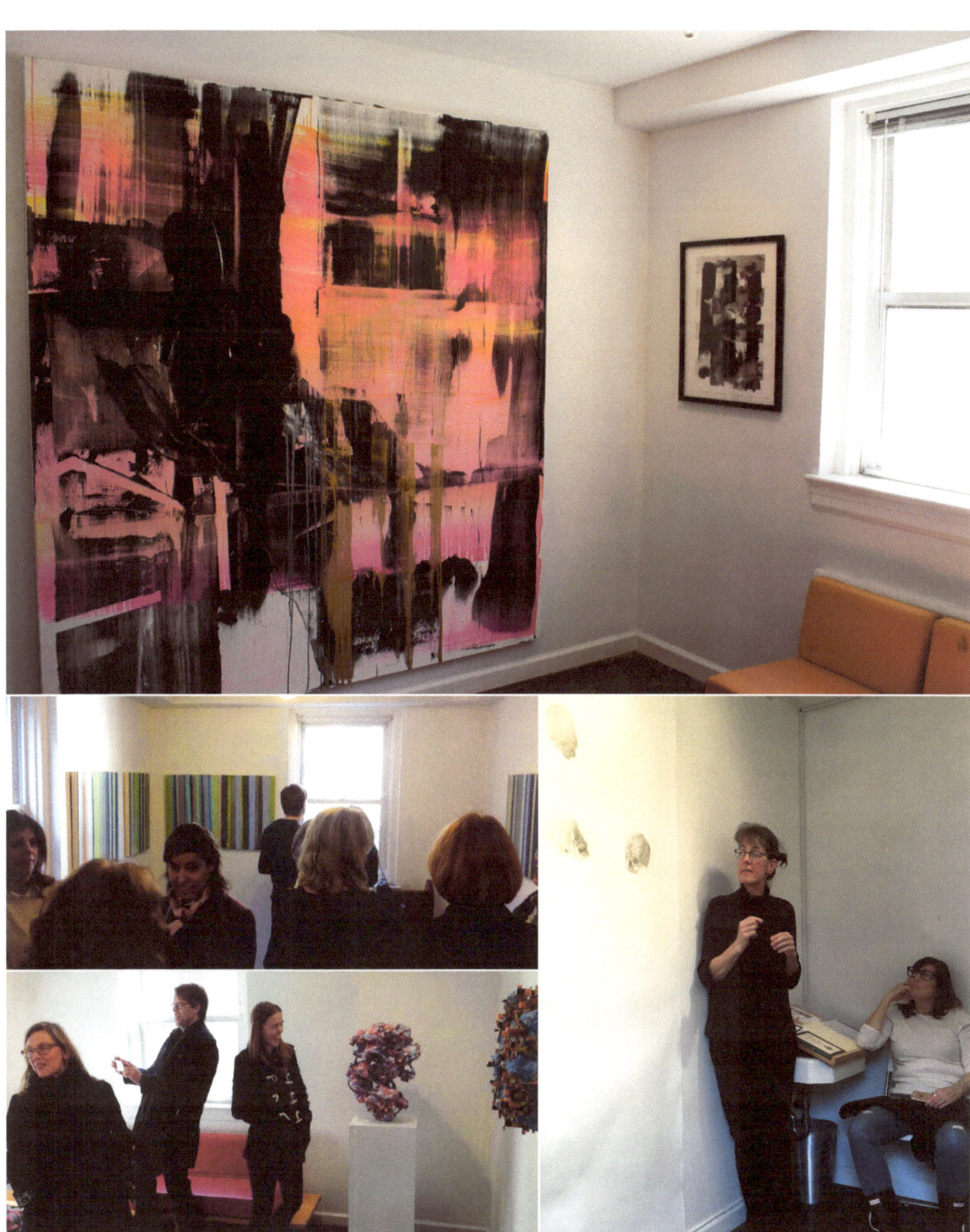

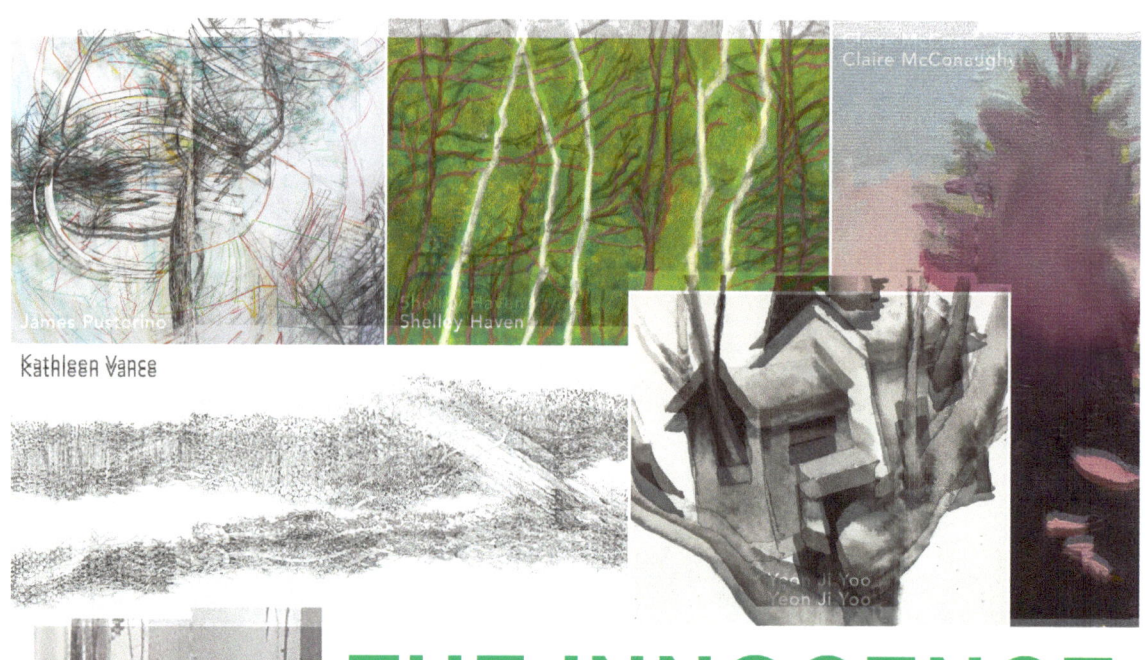

THE INNOCENCE OF TREES

Curated by Anne Trauben

EXHIBITION: Friday 04/21/17 - Saturday 06/10/17
ARTIST RECEPTION: Sunday, April 23rd, 2017, 3-6p
WORKSHOP/TALK: Sat 05/06 & Sun 05/07, 3-6p
CLOSING PARTY: Sat 6/10/17, 3-6p

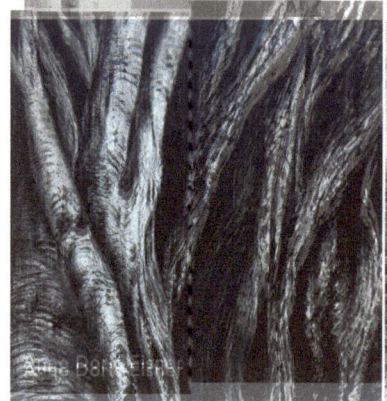
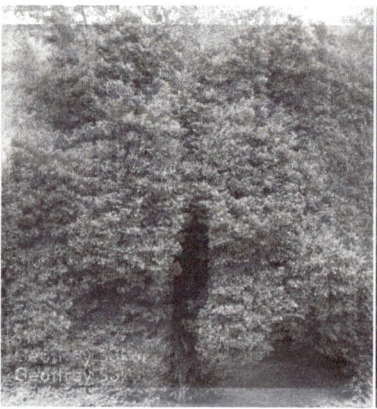
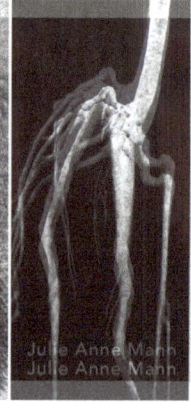
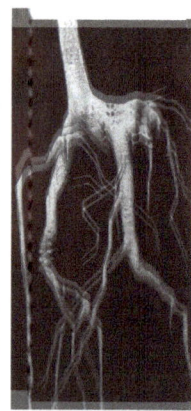

The Innocence of Trees is a group show featuring drawing, painting, photography, sculpture and installation by nine artists in 9 gallery rooms: Anne Doris-Eisner, Claire McConaughy, Dana Scott, Geoffrey Sokol, James Pusterino, Julie Anne Mann, Kathleen Vance, Shelley Haven and Yeon Ji Yoo, who create works which focus on a study of trees. The show is curated by Anne Trauben.

Drawing Rooms will be a forest during Earth Day, Arbor Day and all through May as we celebrate our love of Planet Earth. This is our second show of the year in response to the new administration. The title of the exhibit, The Innocence of Trees, is borrowed from Agnes Martin, who said when she first made a grid, she happened to be thinking of the innocence of trees.

Anne Doris-Eisner's imposing, life-size black and white tree trunk drawings are made with a tactile and strenuous process of mark making. For painter **Claire McConaughy**, the forms and

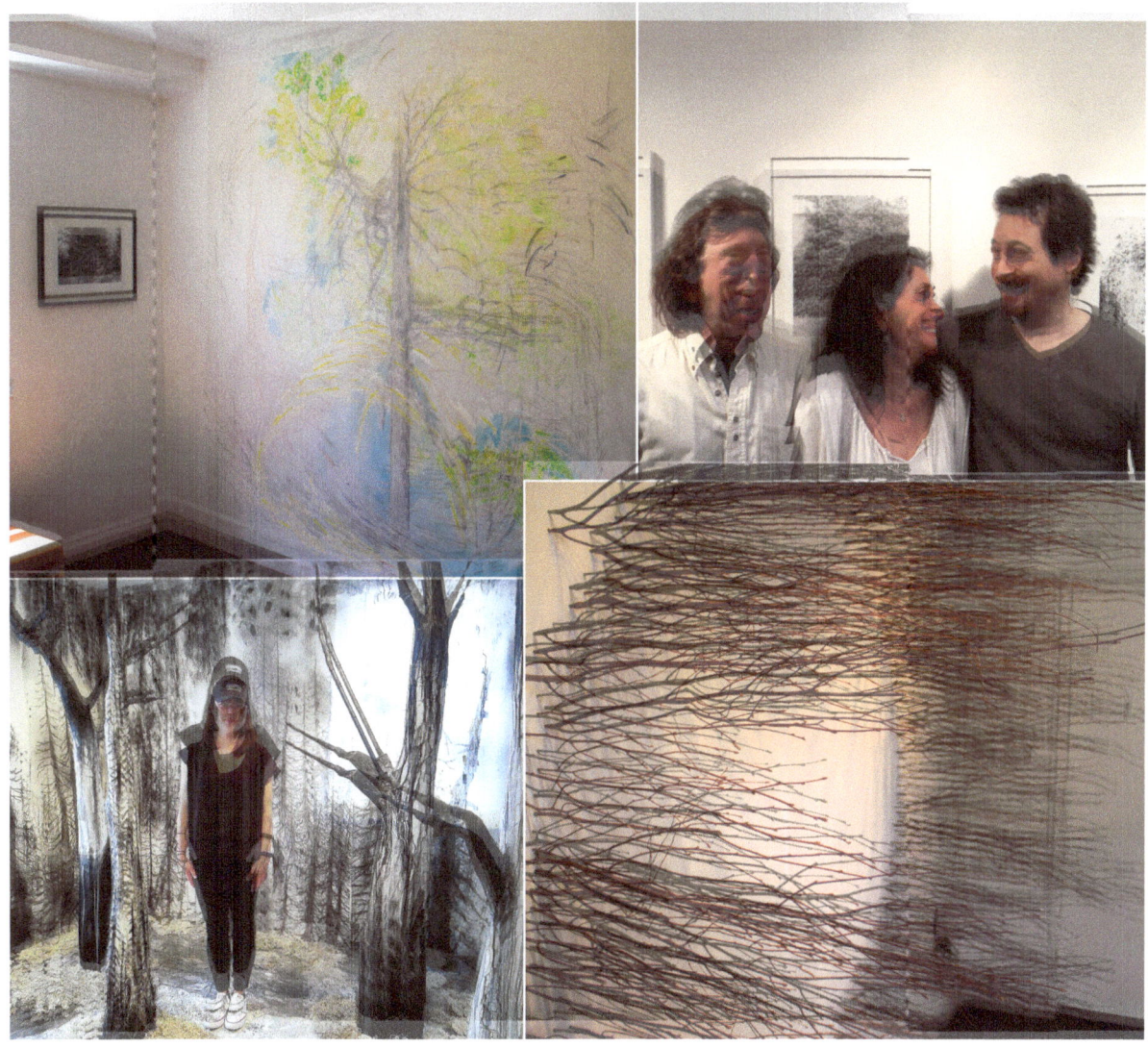

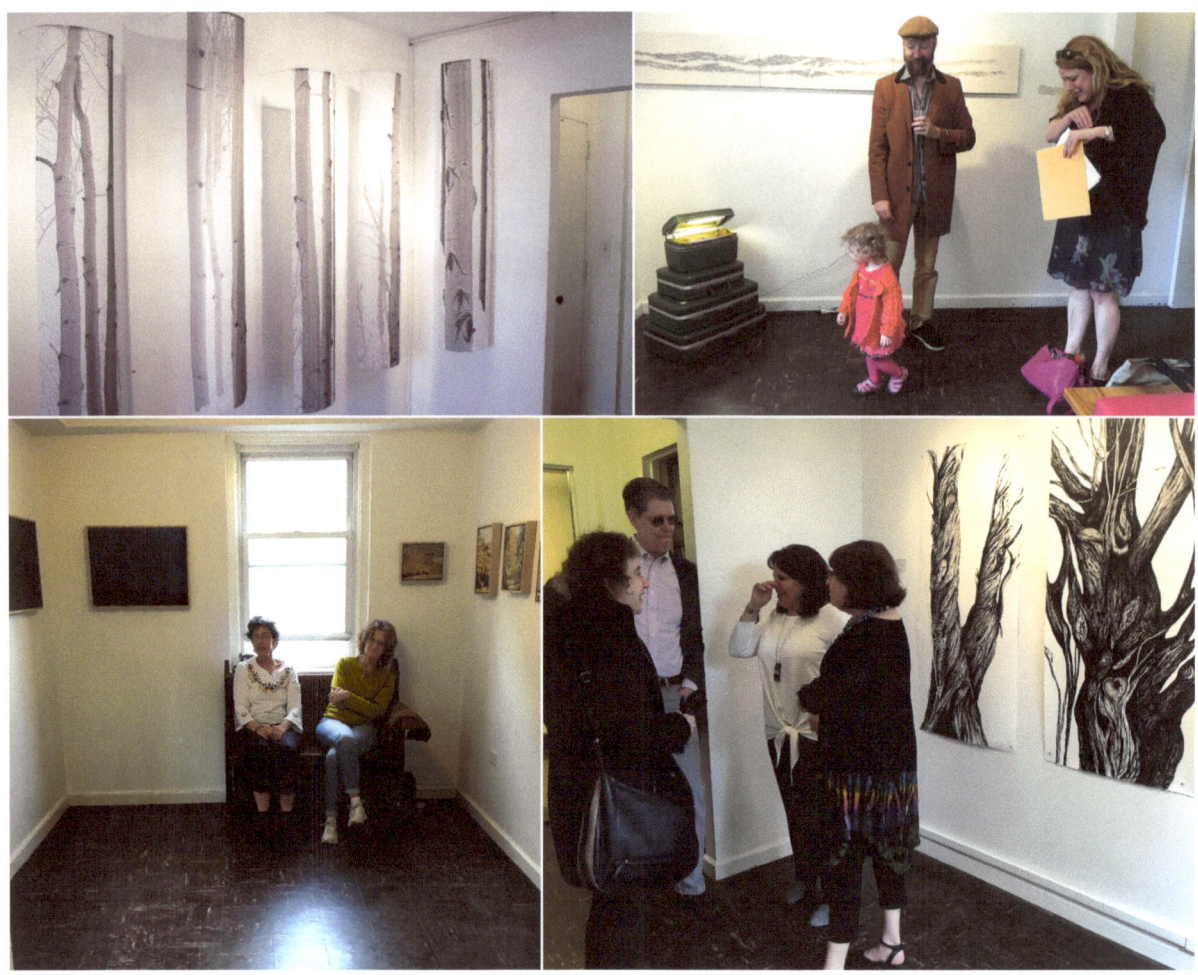

tones of a scene are adjusted until they are new moments poetically composed. In **Dana Scott's** installation, Ghost Forest, the quiet austerity of trees is emphasized by the repetition of simple form, both throughout the space and within the images, while the translucent material evokes the mysterious beauty of the forest. **Geoffrey Sokol** photographs trees for the peacefulness he feels walking among them. The images, taken in woods, forests, and urban parks and gardens are both real, 'suggestions' and possibilities, created using digital and darkroom techniques. **James Pustorino's** large, detailed drawings, attempt to capture the movement of individual trees and the space around them. A circle of branches appear to come straight out of the wall in **Julie Anne Mann's** 'Threshold'. In her "Traveling Landscapes", **Kathleen Vance** creates miniature landscapes inside vintage suitcases and trunks. Painter **Shelly Haven** builds delicate layers of paint that reveal the mood and story of the land and invite quiet meditation. **Yeon Ji Yoo** creates an installation where inky wash pines, tall trees and moss underfoot create a forest dreamland as she reaches back into childhood remembrances of her life in Korea.

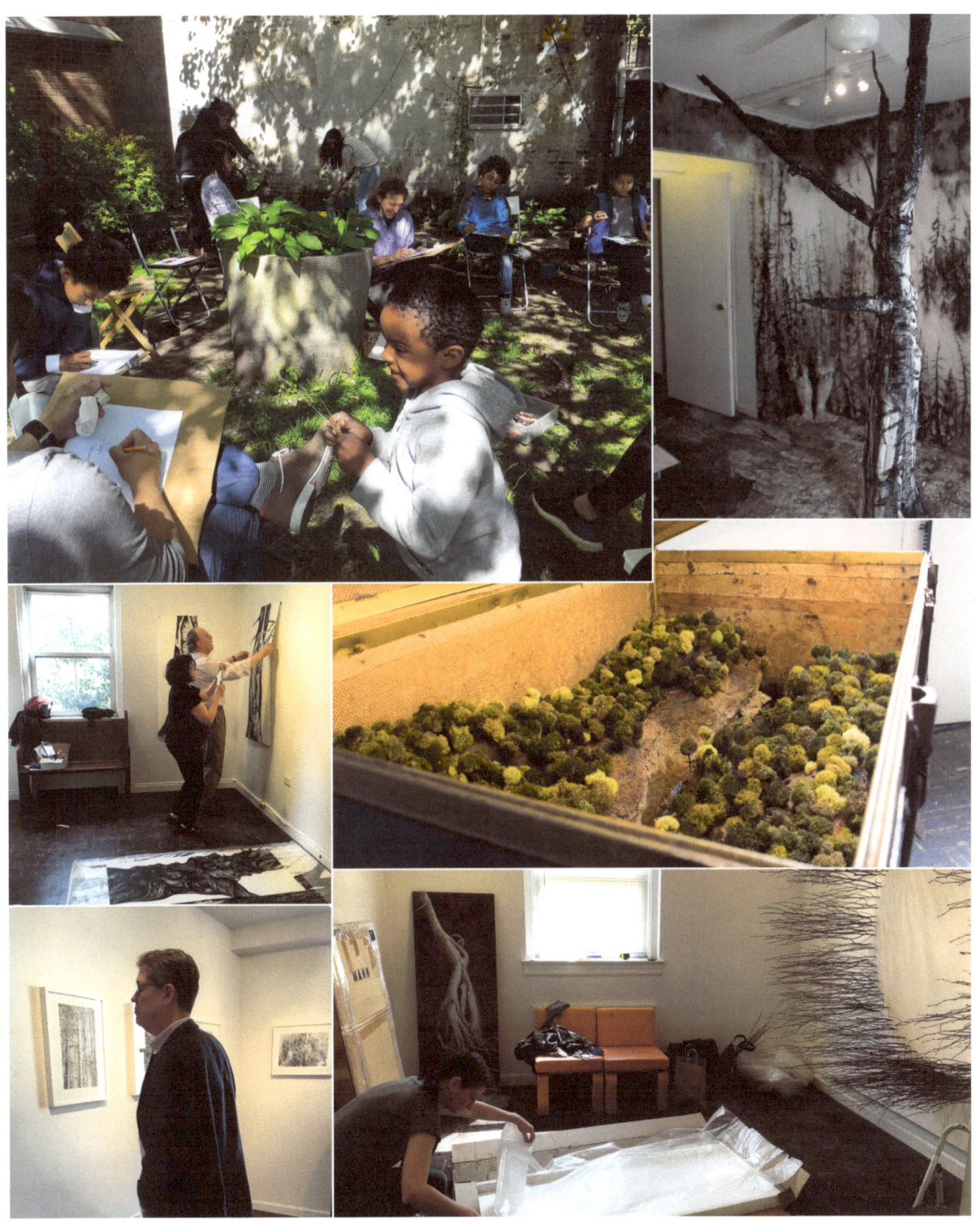

33   The Innocence of Trees

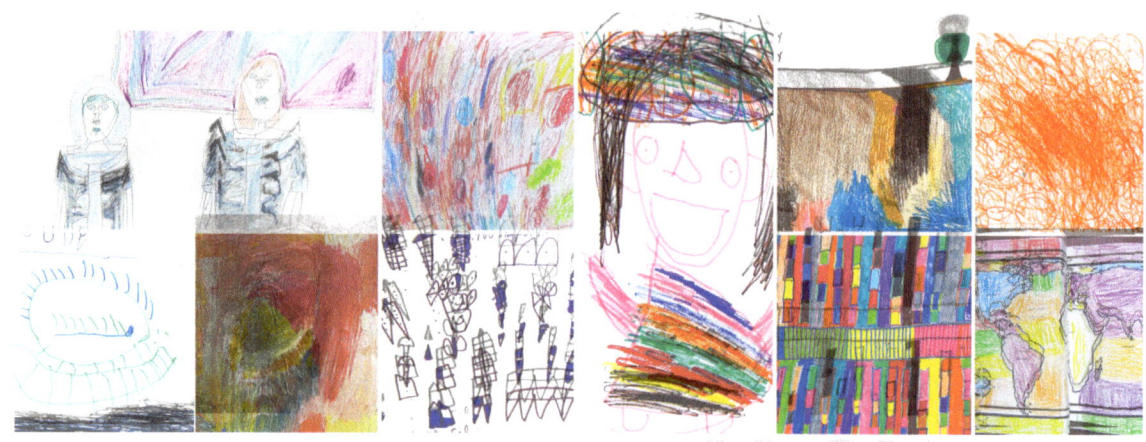

THE CAN-MAN SHOW

EXHIBITION: Thursday 06/22/17 - Saturday 07/22/17 **RECEPTION:** Sunday, June 25th, 2017, 3-6p

OUTSIDER ART FUNDRAISER: Thursday, June 22nd, 2017 6-9p

Rainbow Thursdays Director: Jill Scipione / Curator: Anne Trauben

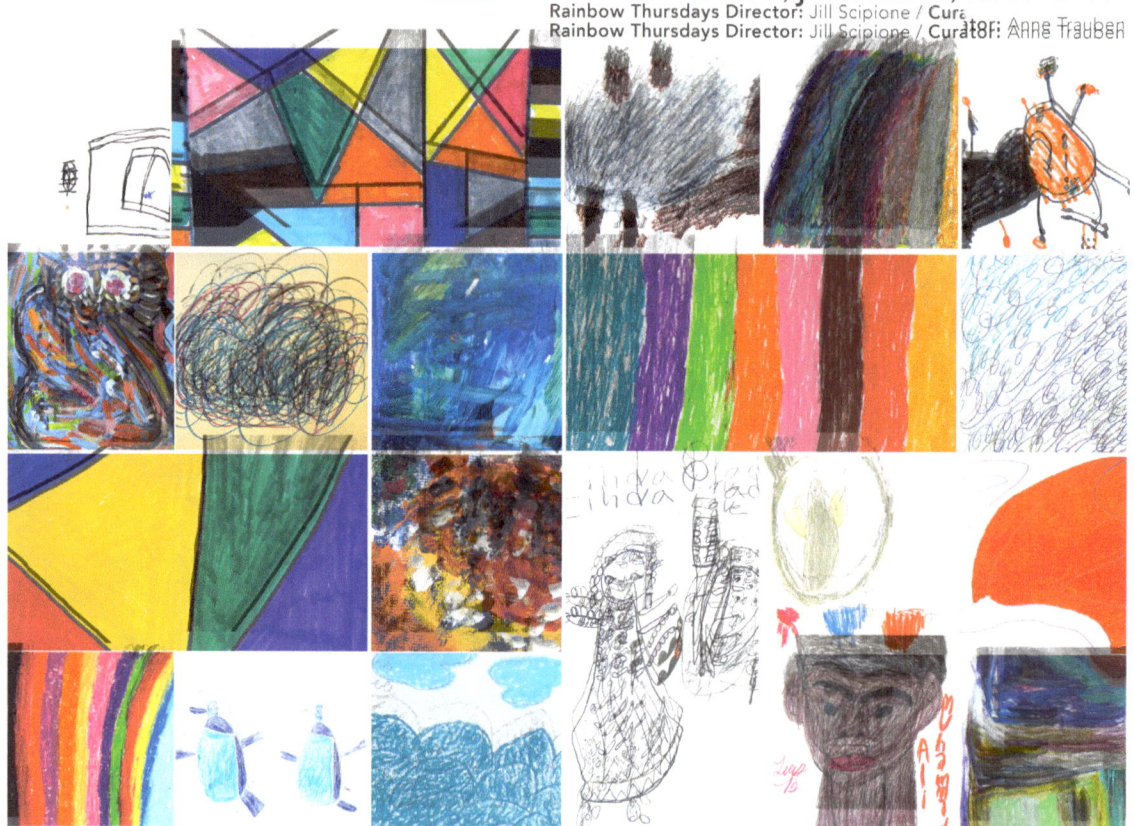

The Can-Man Show is an exhibition of works by Rainbow Thursdays artists, Victory Hall Inc.'s weekly art program for developmentally disabled artists. The selection of paintings and drawings in The Can-Man Show is the culmination of almost five years of Rainbow Thursdays artist's works. Each artist may have very varying capabilities, but everyone participates enthusiastically and many come up with surprising results.

Aida works from early Christian icons and Renaissance paintings in books and mass cards and translates devotional imagery into simple, flat space and symbol. Alan draws ordinary scenes: city hall, the Bayonne bridge, local schools, trees and playgrounds, and makes poem drawings and crossword puzzles about these subjects. Charles can draw anything put in front of him and change it into a happy scene, give it his trademark big smile. Cheryl sees pattern in nature. Her work has a graphic quality, stylizing the elements of nature. Debbie brings her direct, thoughtful sense of order and gentle sense of color to all she does. Christopher's work has a conceptual basis and his imagery is often iconic or symbolic. His word pieces that are portraits of alternative personas. Dennis likes drawing helicopters, boats, bridges, mountains, whales, buildings, trees and finds relationships between forms and colors. Dina's work is very gestural and kinetic. Her subjects are hearts, flowers and seasonal themes - Christmas trees, Easter baskets, or snowmen. Ed's artwork is a vast array of images and shapes, some drawn

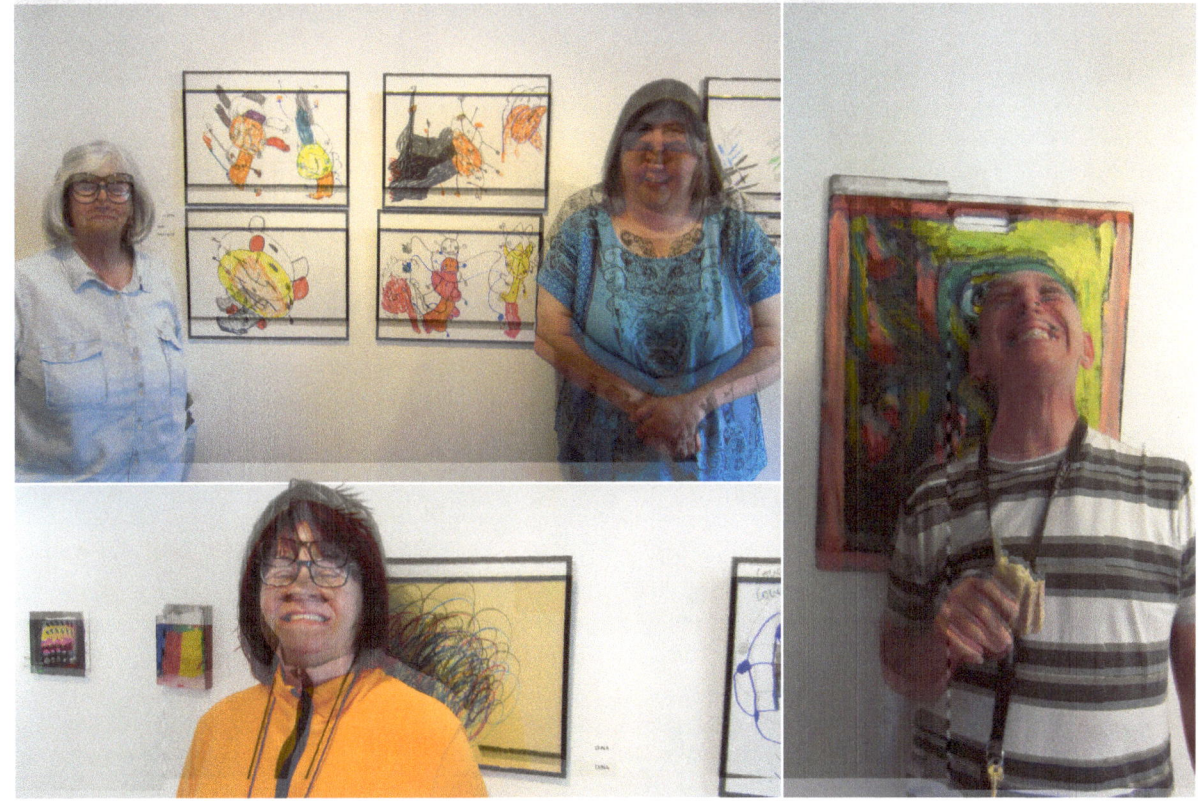

35 The Can-Man Show

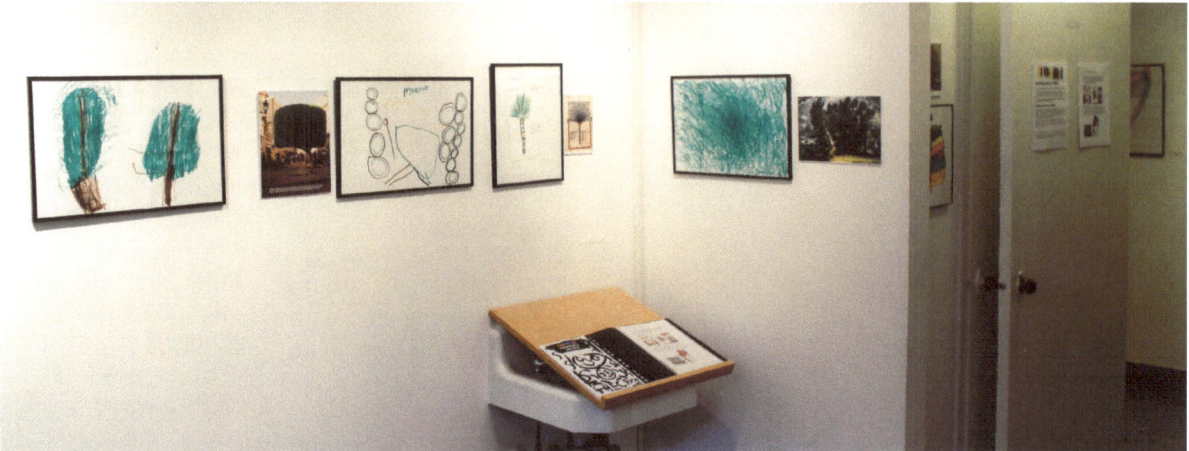

from his mind and others from photographs or his response to artworks. **Eric** draws from books of paintings or photos of his favorite television stars, and strives to get a good likeness. **Eugene** has an innate sense of color and form. His brilliant shapes of pure color do not obviously refer to anything he is looking at. **Hirra's** drawings engage writing and symbol-making. She draws tents, churches, houses and people, with crosses scattered everywhere. **Jimmy** makes smooth, looping lines as if they were drawn while listening to music. **Jude's** pictures consist of emblematic imagery: a clock, a person, a house, as well as hearts and shamrocks; his spindly, electrified line that enlivens the forms. **Judy's** dancing hares, floating dragonflies, leaping dolphins are animated by her blocks of color juxtaposed with her delicate linework. **Kaitlyn** creates her own kaleidoscopic assemblies of lines and ribbons of color that she arranges like musical notes. **Linda** takes inspiration from the style of coloring books. She draws with an emphatic outline to be later colored in. **Louis** works from images he finds on his phone or in print, from pop-culture, black history, advertising, animals, indigenous art and other sources that come to his mind. **Luis** constructs his paintings out of fluid lines and painterly washes of colors. He uses letters, numbers and words as pictorial elements. **Marcello** thinks carefully about his color choices and the order, width and intensity of each band in his rainbow drawings. **Mary Beth** draws with a cartoonist's sure sense of line and quick confidence. Her subjects, schmoos, are almost always a mix of right-side up and upside down parts. **Michael** works in coloring books, overriding the images underneath and fills the images with colors and creates a color composition that works outside or against the lines of the picture. **Mina's** drawing is an activity, an expression of the motion and energy that he has within himself, as well as of the physical limitations he has to deal with. **Nicky** draws cruise ships, dinosaurs, camels climbing hills of sand in the desert, and blimps. He draws with emphatic speed. **Nicole's** blends of tones and hues, and her use of brush strokes to activate and build-up the texture of her paintings, is sophisticated and beautifully achieved. **Noreen** draws in layers, often making a kind of face first and then layering over it with drawn colors, sometimes adding paint on top of that. **Paulette** works very intensely, laying color line over color line and building up an often dense progression of drawn tone and texture as her way to communicate. **Sal** draws from an inner graphic language of shapes, line and words and inscribes and dedicates each one to the person to whom he gives the drawing to. **Timothy's** drawings begin with photographs of girls that he may know or may like to know. His paintings are colorfully patterned interpretations of pictures he sees. **Wayne** experiments with color and paint. His world is filled with happy monsters, people turning into butterflies, happy bugs, and Chinese soup. **Wendy's** paintings have a dramatic, energetic contrast of colors and explosive bursts of dark and bright hues. **Yahira's** landscape pictures are luminous arrangements of tones and textures using colored pencils, markers, watercolor paint, oil pastels and crayons, often in the same picture.

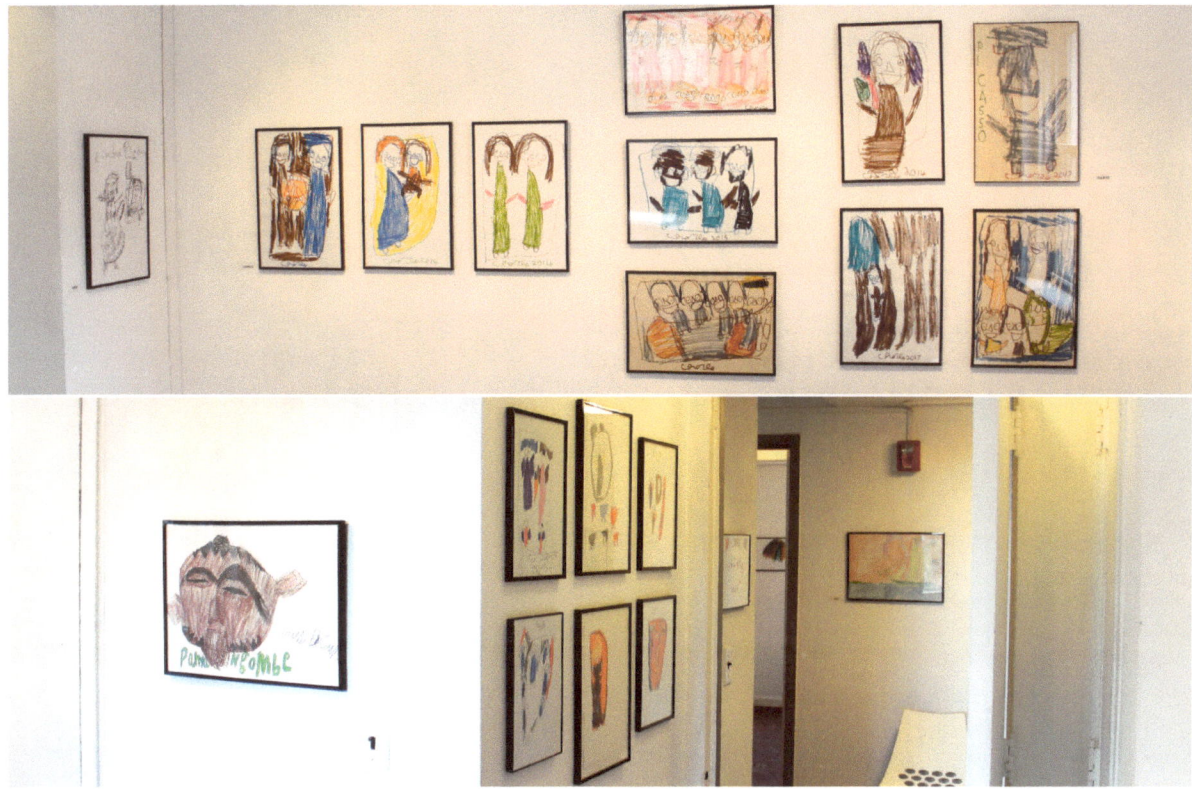

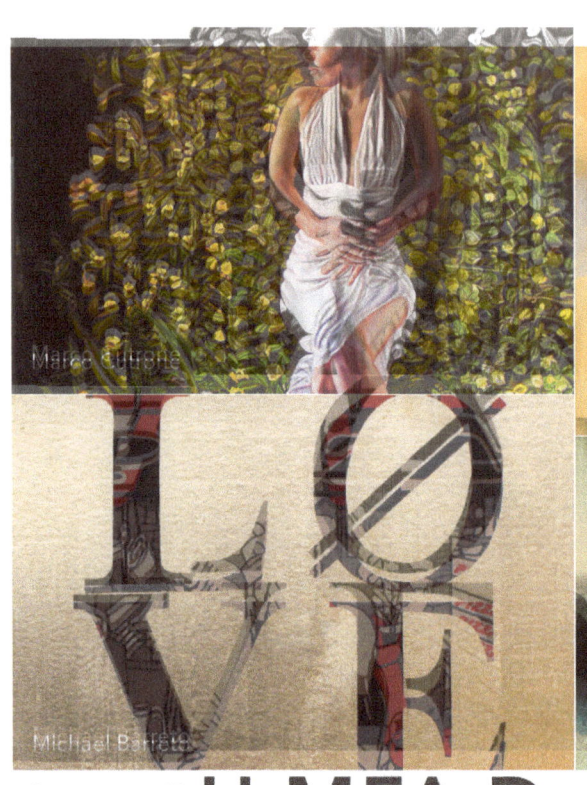
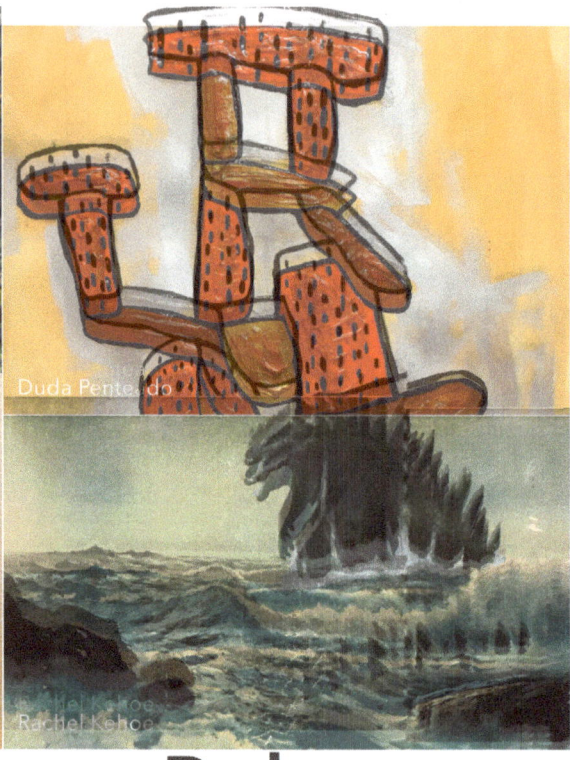

NJCU MFA Dress Rehearsal

Friday, July 28th to Saturday, August 12th, 2017 / Curated by Anne Trauben

Artist Reception: Saturday 7/29/17, 3-8p
Workshop/Talk: Saturday 8/5 & Sunday 8/6, 3-6p
Closing Party: Saturday 8/12/17, 3-8p

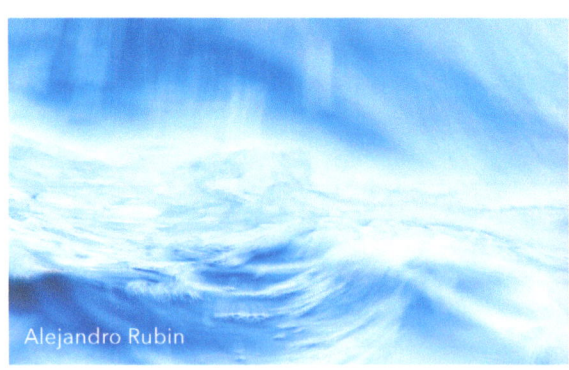
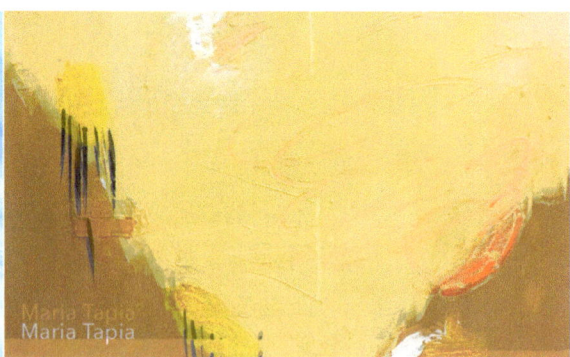

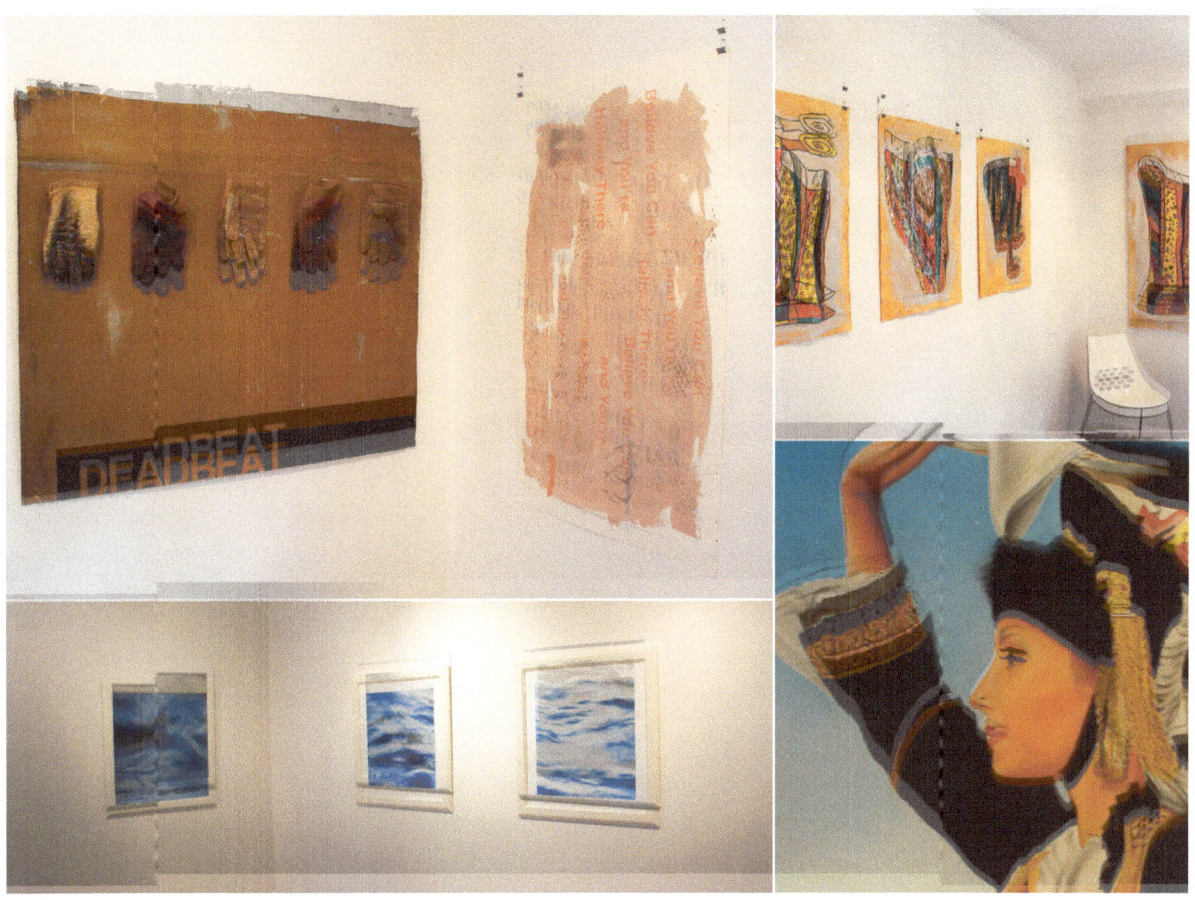

NJCU MFA Dress Rehearsal is a group show featuring drawing, painting, photography, sculpture and installation by six NJCU MFA students in 7 gallery rooms: Alejandro Rubin, Duda Penteado, Marco Cutrone, Maria Tapia, Michael Barreto, and Rachel Kehoe. The show is curated by Anne Trauben.

Alejandro Rubin's photo installation in two rooms invites the viewer to interact with a body of water and share in his experience of being immersed. In Duda Penteado's Layers and Pieces series, he investigates the track of human evolution through various cultures. Maria Tapia's vibrant, luminous paintings become personal metaphors for a turbulent world of light and deep darkness, invoking magic and spiritual traditions. Michael Barreto's graphic pop imagery explores concepts of consumerism, conformity and mass production affecting society and what it means to be an individual. Rachel Kehoe adds pop imagery and art historical references to "kitsch"; banal paintings in order "to elevate them and bring them out of the dusty thrift store and into contemporary times." Marco Cutrone's pencil drawings and paintings portray women in various poses and settings which explore concepts of fashion and glamour and perceptions of beauty and strength in current culture.

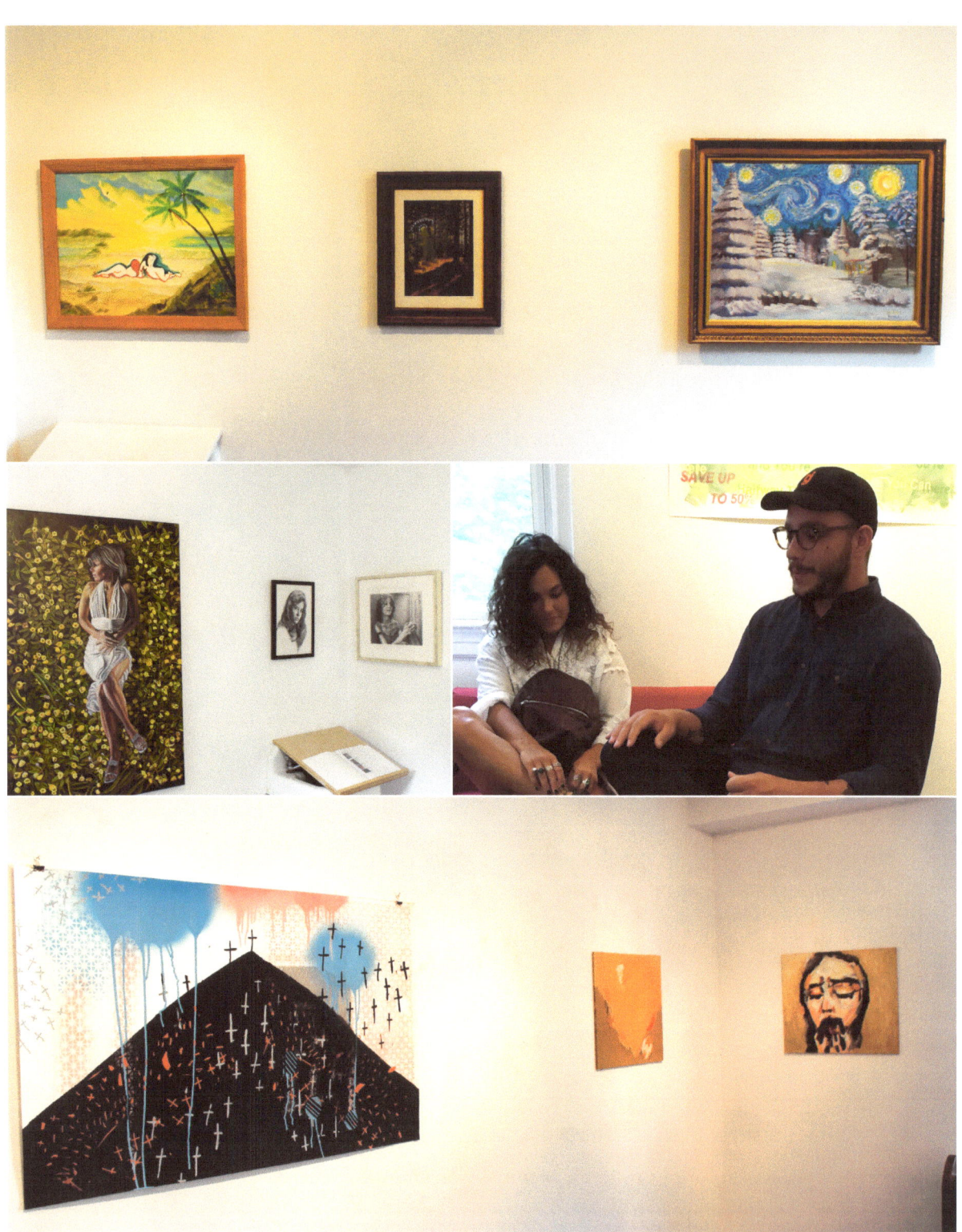

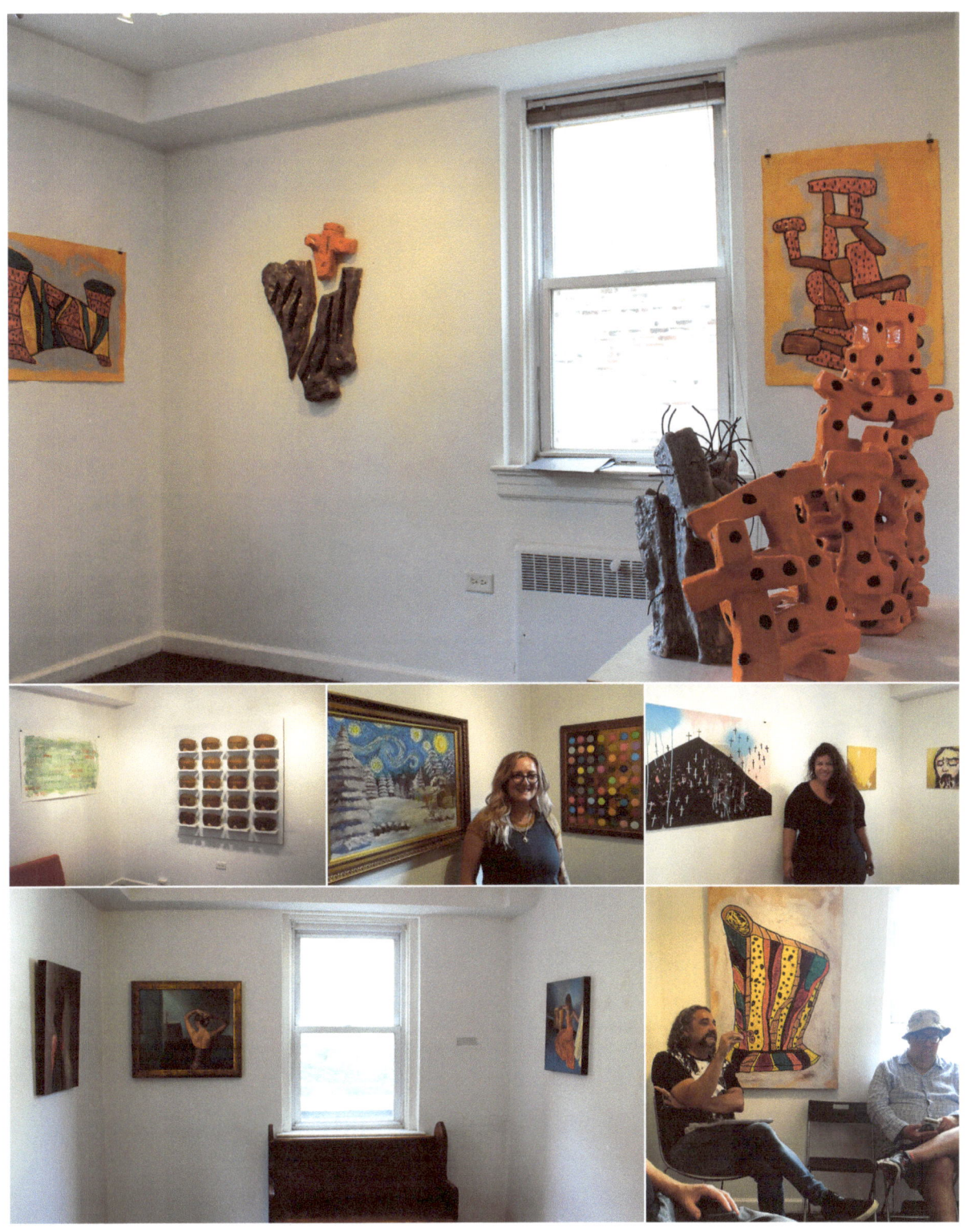

41 NJCU MFA Dress Rehearsal

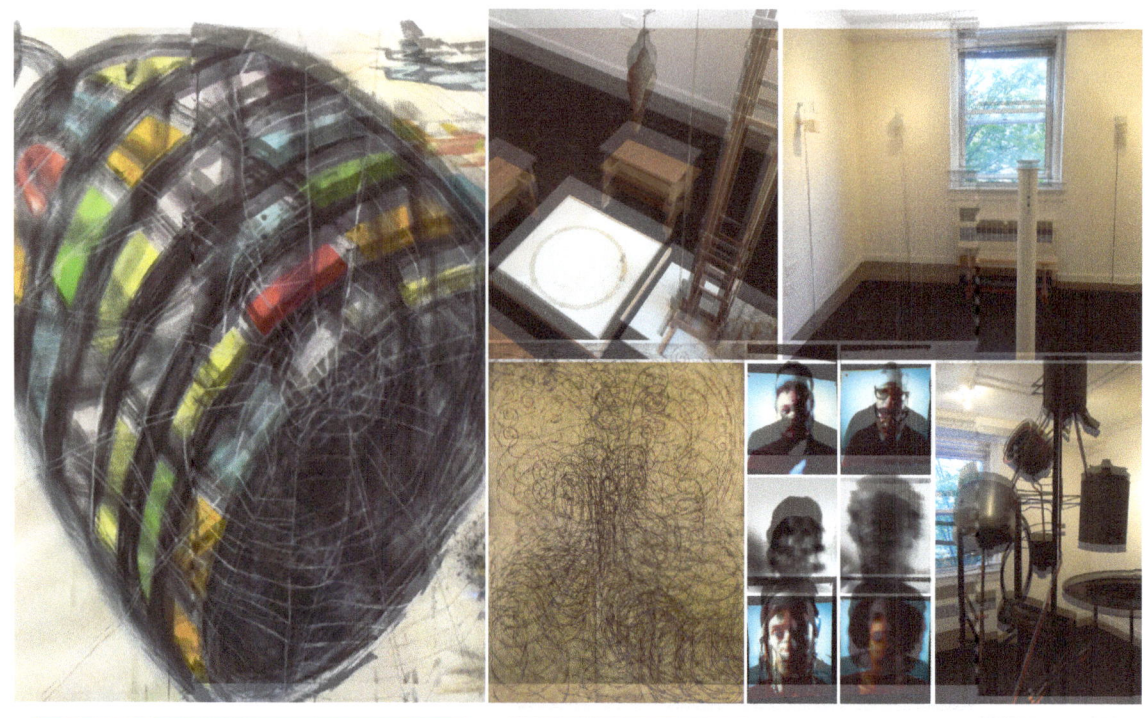

■ HONORING MARGARET: THE WORK OF MARGARET WEBER

■ SUP-A-GENIUS: THE FIVE GUY SHOW

Artist in Show: Anthony Fisher, Kurt Steger, John Morton*, Joe Chirchirillo, and Roger Sayre

*John Morton received a Foundation for Contemporary Arts Emergency Grant for his work in the show.

FRIDAY, SEPTEMBER 22ND TO SATURDAY, NOVEMBER 11TH, 2017
Shows Curated by Anne Trauben

HONORING MARGARET & SUP-A-GENIUS Reception:
Sunday, September 24th, 2017 from 3:00pm to 6:00pm

SUP-A-GENIUS Workshops / Talks:
Saturday, October 7th, & Sunday, October 8th, 2017 from 3:00pm to 6:00pm

JC Artist Studio Tour:
Saturday, October 14th, & Sunday, October 15th, 2017 from 12:00pm to 6:00pm

Closing Party:
Saturday, November 11th, 2017 from 3:00pm to 6:00pm

The Fall season at Drawing Rooms opened with two exhibitions: a collection of works by a beloved Jersey City artist and community leader, and five gallery rooms featuring artists who have each created unusually intriguing mechanical and interactive systems which produce their art. The exhibitions are curated by Anne Trauben.

Honoring Margaret: The Work of Margaret Weber is a mini-retrospective of works by Margaret Weber, a long-time Jersey City resident, art pioneer, arts organizer, mother, sister, local activist, teacher, co-founder of Drawing Rooms and friend to so many. This posthumous exhibit, produced with the help of her daughter Zoe, features drawing, painting, prints and collage works made by Margaret during the course of her lifetime. Margaret Weber's work looks deeply into the human soul and our earthly condition, exploring both joy and darkness. Her bold, expressive imagery is boundless in its range. Figures move through broken spaces, skulls, helicopters, ravens and owls interact with symbols such as hands, eyes, and letter-forms that all tell a mysterious, urgent, tale. This vital sense of purpose marked her life in her community as well. Of her own work, she wrote: " I am pessimistic about the current state of human interaction with the natural world.... A compelling, even beautiful picture of an ugly reality develops. This image might move one to feel, think, act. Hopefully. "

Sup-A-Genius: The Five Guy Show is an exhibition that celebrates the artist as inventor. The works of the "five guys" in this show engage the creation of a situation, condition, or home-made machine or contraption that actually

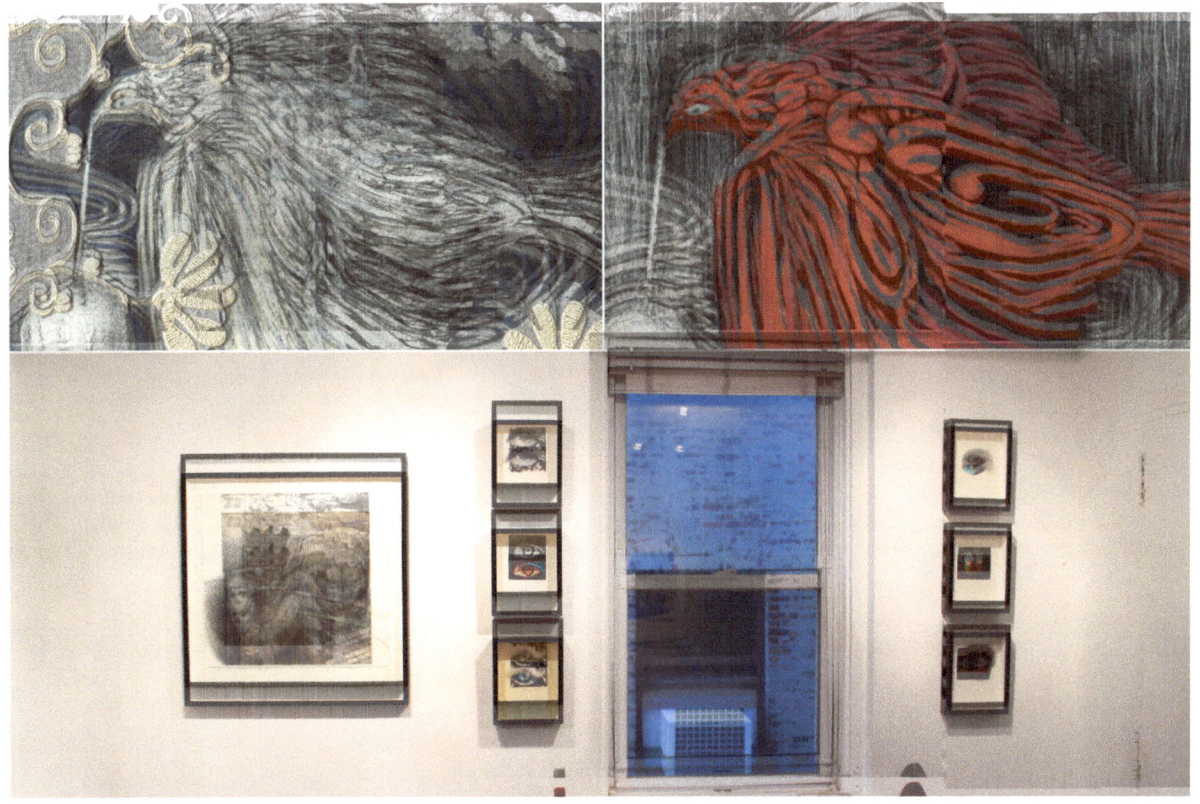

43 Honoring Margaret: The Work of Margaret Weber

creates the art. The art moves, responds to human presence, requires viewer interaction to be made, or is made through specific conditions set up by the artist. Sup-A-Genius features works by Anthony Fisher, Kurt Steger, John Morton, Joe Chirchirillo, Roger Sayre. John Morton's work is sponsored in-part by a Foundation for Contemporary Arts Emergency Grant.

Boston-area artist, **Anthony Fisher's** "Turbulence" drawings are made by an intense physical process that involves the artist pushing wheeled carts loaded with masonry and dragging construction tools laden with weights across paper laid on the floor, over and over again to create interwound patterns of ink and charcoal. He then layers spray paint on the paper, and sometimes stamps cut reeds and straw into the surface by walking over it. Fisher's evocative drawings are made through this self-imposed mechanical system, like an ancient mythic labor. **Kurt Steger's** "Meltdown" invites participants to interact with his structure that suspends ice above a sheet of paper. As they rotate the paper, the melting ice drips, creating a Zen-like circle of 'urban stains' that is surprisingly beautiful. Mixed into the ice are materials such as carbon, rust, soil, and locally harvested toxic waters. **Roger Sayre's** "Sitting" combines primitive photography with meditation, collaboration and endurance. Visitors can sign-up to sit in front of his custom-made pinhole camera that fills half the gallery room, and meditate on their own image in a mirror mounted on the front of the camera for the duration of the hour-long exposure. Long-time Jersey City artist **Joe Chirchirillo** returns from Vermont for an installation of his "Sculpture Systems". These kinetic pieces are powered by small electric motors, pumps or sometimes by hand and draw their inspiration from natural cycles. Contrasting nature with the man-made, they create a "false nature", re-created in an absurd mechanized fashion. Composer and artist **John Morton's** 'Fever Songs' is an interactive public sound installation project that brings together the vocal traditions of many religions, creating an active sonic experience which explores spiritual commonality and seeks to break down religious divisions. As the audience wanders in the space, sensors will record and control various aspects of the audio output. The actual sonic choices will be chosen randomly, and then woven together, harmonized, commingled and overlapped by computer.

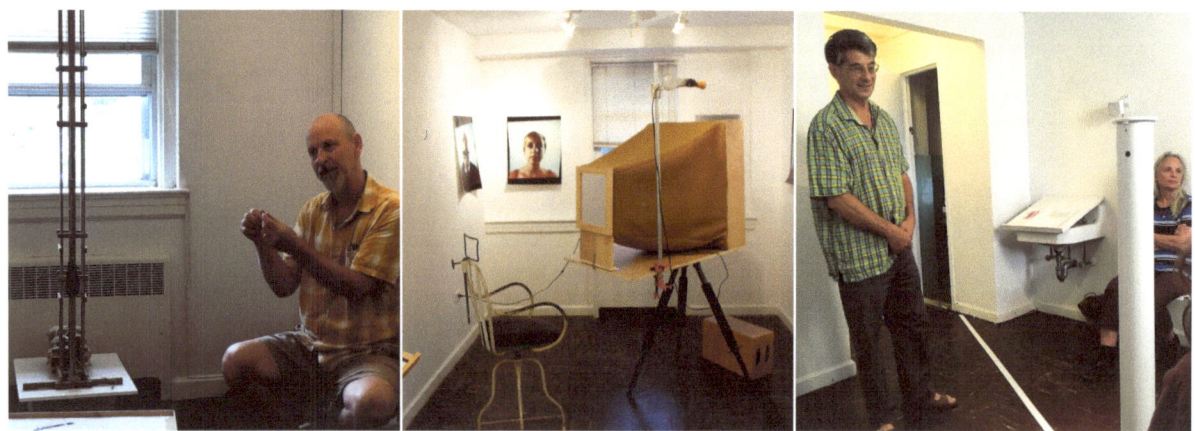

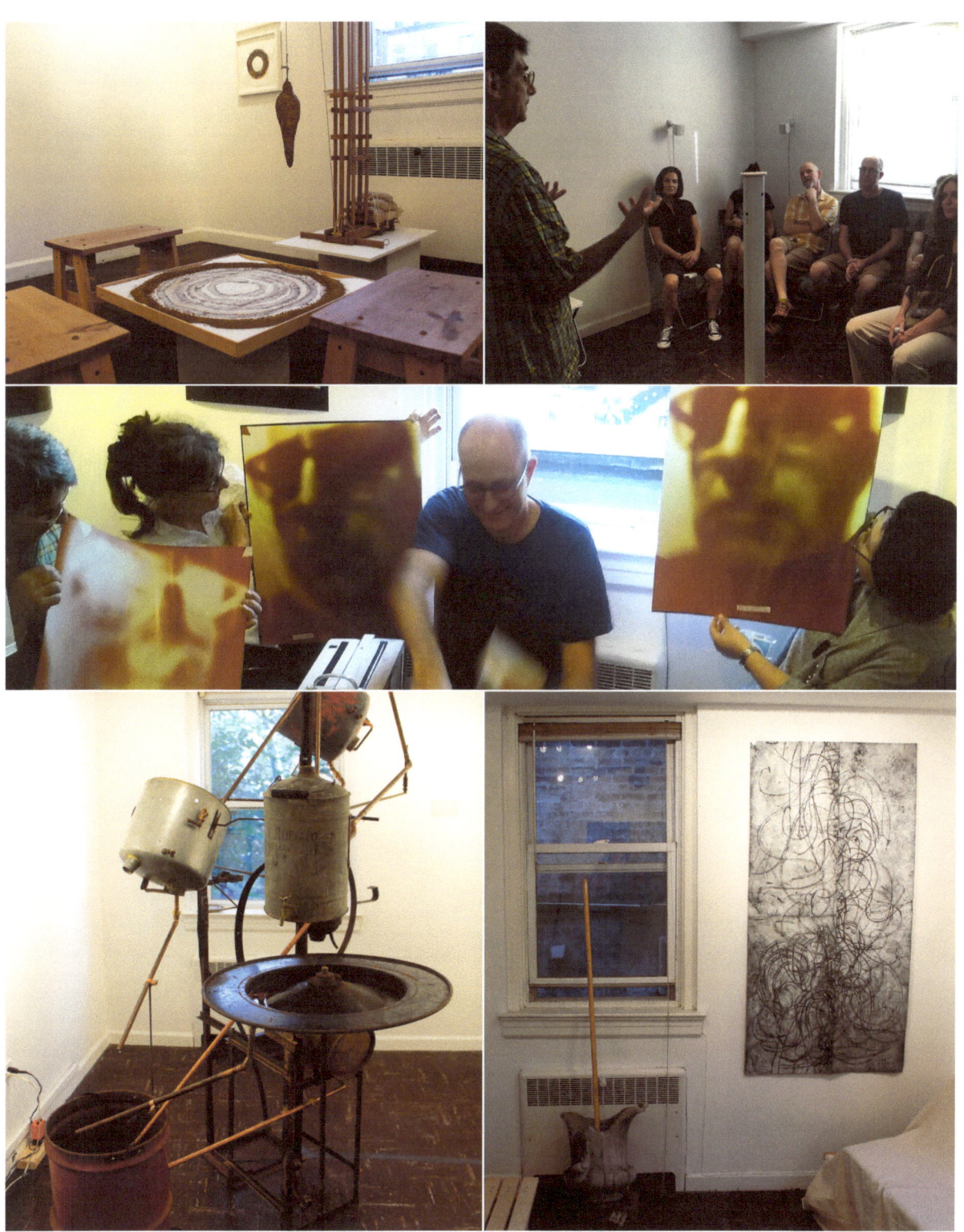

45 Honoring Margaret: The Work of Margaret Weber

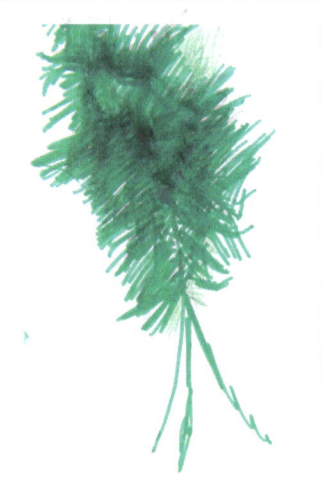
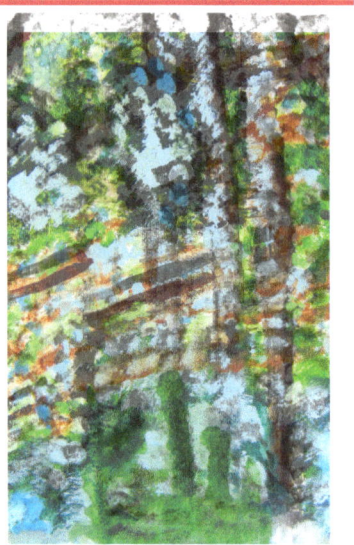
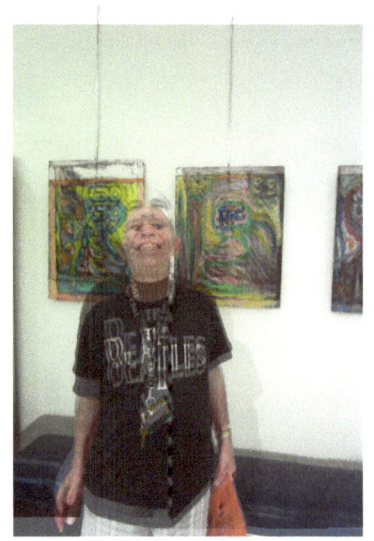
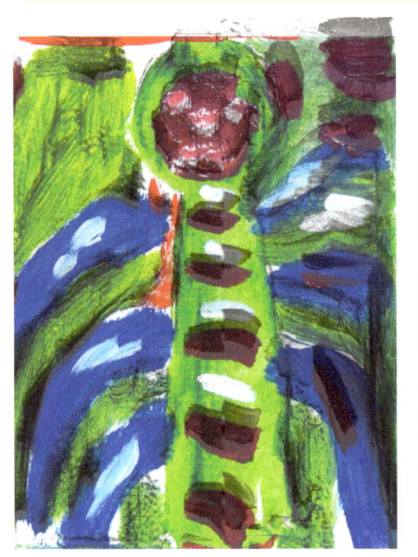
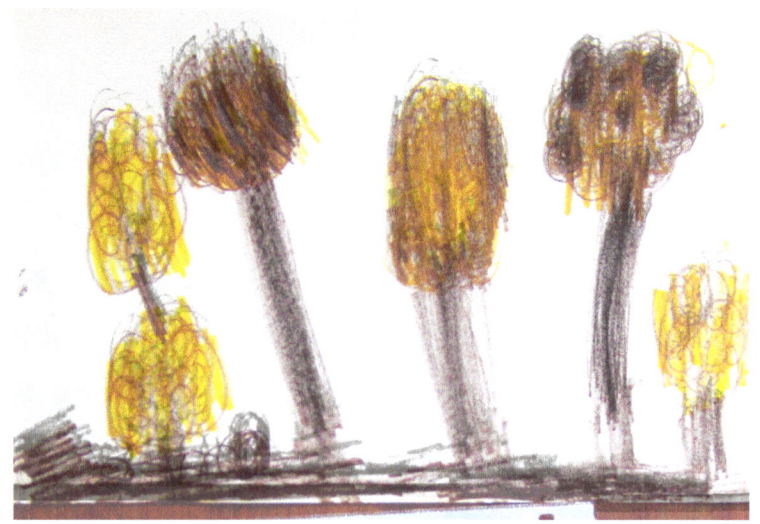
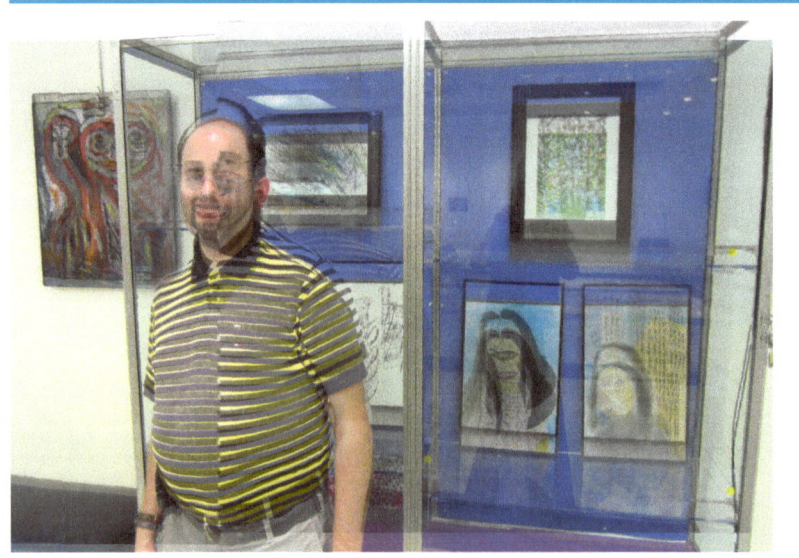
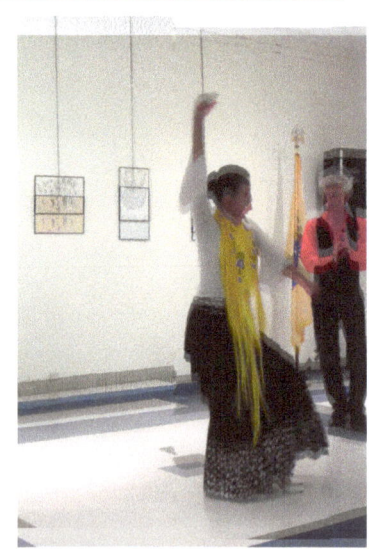

RAINBOW THURSDAYS ARTISTS

Rainbow Thursdays Artists is our community-based art education program connecting disabled adults with professional artists who provide them with materials, training and encouragement to express themselves through art. High school students interested in art also visit as assistants. These classes are presented free of charge, and are funded in part by a CDBG grant from the City of Bayonne.

This weekly outreach art program in cooperation with Windmill Alliance, is now in its fourth full year of operation and many of our participants are advancing in their creativity and skills and are developing an identity as an artist.

About forty program participants meet weekly to learn painting and drawing with three to four artist/teachers at Windmill Center for developmentally disabled adults, 5th and Broadway, Bayonne, NJ. Up to twenty visiting artists from the NJ/NY area also meet with the students and share their artwork and instruction.

The program encompasses study of great artworks, the natural world, and images of people through books and photographs, and encourages each participant to understand drawing as their unique visual language with which they can create realistic and abstract form and systems, and express emotion and ideas through line and color. The population at Windmill may have very varying capabilities, but that only adds to their individual artistic statement and everyone participates enthusiastically and many come up with surprising results.

We also organize exhibitions throughout the year for our Rainbow Artists to share and show their work both at our Drawing Rooms location and at community spaces throughout the area. This year featured two exhibits, one at Drawing Rooms in Spring and one at the he Bayonne Public Library in Fall. The opportunity to exhibit and even sell their artwork to family, friends and many supporters in the community allows our Rainbow Artists to become visible and valued in a new way.

ARTISTS WORK SPACES

The Artist's' Work-space Program at Drawing Rooms, on our third floor, has become an important part our art center's activities at our 180 Grand Street location.

Now that the work of renovation on the third floor of our former convent building is done, artists who form the core of our organization are able to rent studios and share their work with the public during Open Studio weekends throughout the year.

A great addition to our second floor exhibition rooms, the Work-spaces create a place where artists can work together and invite the public into the art-making process.

Artists for 2017/18 include: Jill Scipione, Anne Trauben, Maggie Ens, Diane Tenerelli, Candy le Sueur, Roger Sayre and Gregory Letson.

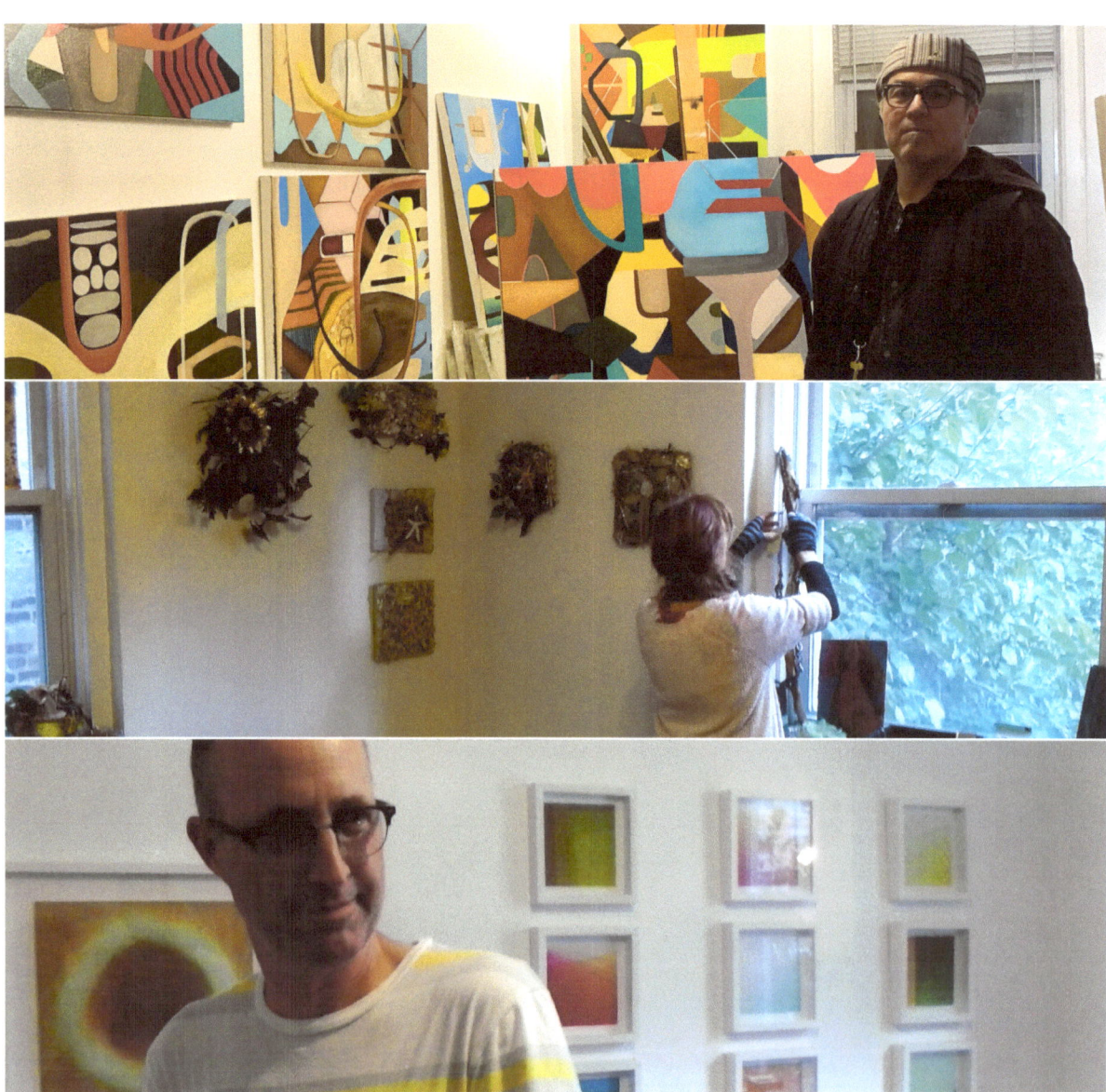

HAND-IN-HAND ART SCHOOL

The Hand-in-Hand program encourages young people to consider themselves artists, both musical and visual, and to see creativity as an important part of their life.

The afterschool program at Grace Lutheran Church Avenue C and 37th St., Bayonne focuses on drawing, painting, collage and sculpture as a basis for exploration of our interior and exterior worlds. The program puts students in touch with professional artists who share their knowledge and work alongside the students. Visiting artists regularly introduce new concepts through one-day workshops both at class time and in our Workshop Festival Days.

Our OPEN DRAWING sessions are inclusive classes focusing on special ed. High School students family and friends.

In this year's program we focused on mosaics and group murals, with teachers Anne Trauben and Kimberley Wiseman.

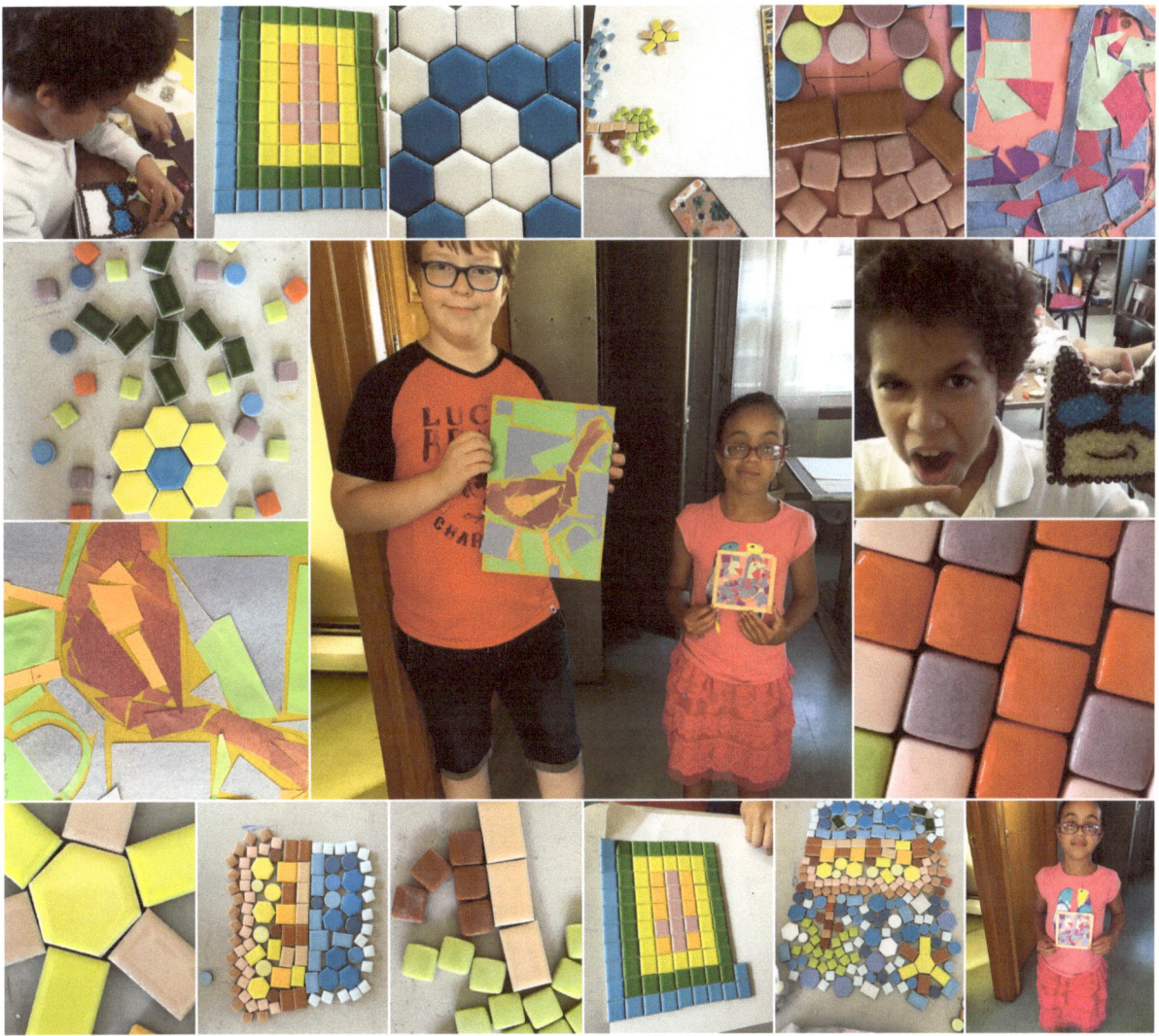

THE ART PROJECT

Victory Hall Inc. Director James Pustorino works throughout the year with Shuster Development, to establish The Art Project in downtown Jersey City. Over thirty-six artists from Jersey City and beyond are currently exhibiting in the forty lobby areas in the four public and residential buildings that the company has built or renovated since 2014.

The goal of this project is to support and promote the artists in Jersey City's Powerhouse Arts District by selling their creations. All proceeds directly benefit the artist, and a meaningful portion goes back into the community, helping to inspire at-risk teenagers through advanced visual arts courses at The Bethune Center in Jersey City's underserved communities.

The buildings are designed to provide viewing areas, lighting and wall space so that each floor acts as an art gallery dedicated to displaying the work of a specific artist. In addition, the expansive space at Gallery 109 Columbus, home of JCity Realty, is open to the public daily and hosts many arts and music events throughout the year. Tours of all lobby-gallery floors in the buildings are given during JC Friday evenings four times a year, and during the Jersey City Studio Tour weekend in October, as well as upon request.

Some of the Showing Artists:
Walter Rodrigues, Deirdre Kennedy, Diane Tenerelli-June, Bruce Halpin, Elaine Hansen, Harriet Finck, Beatrice Mady, Jeannie Gagnon San Chirico, Michael Ensminger, Mona Brody, Robert Egert, Kimberly Wiseman, Anthony Boone, Jodie Fink, Jean-Paul Picard, Roger Sayre, Bill Leech, Alejandro Rubin, Caridad Kennedy, David French, Fukuko Harris, Pat Lay, Susan Evans Grove, Ani Rosskam, Hijo Nam, Karen Nielsen, Szilvia Revesz, Injoo Whang, Kerry Kolenut, Jean-Antoine Norbert.

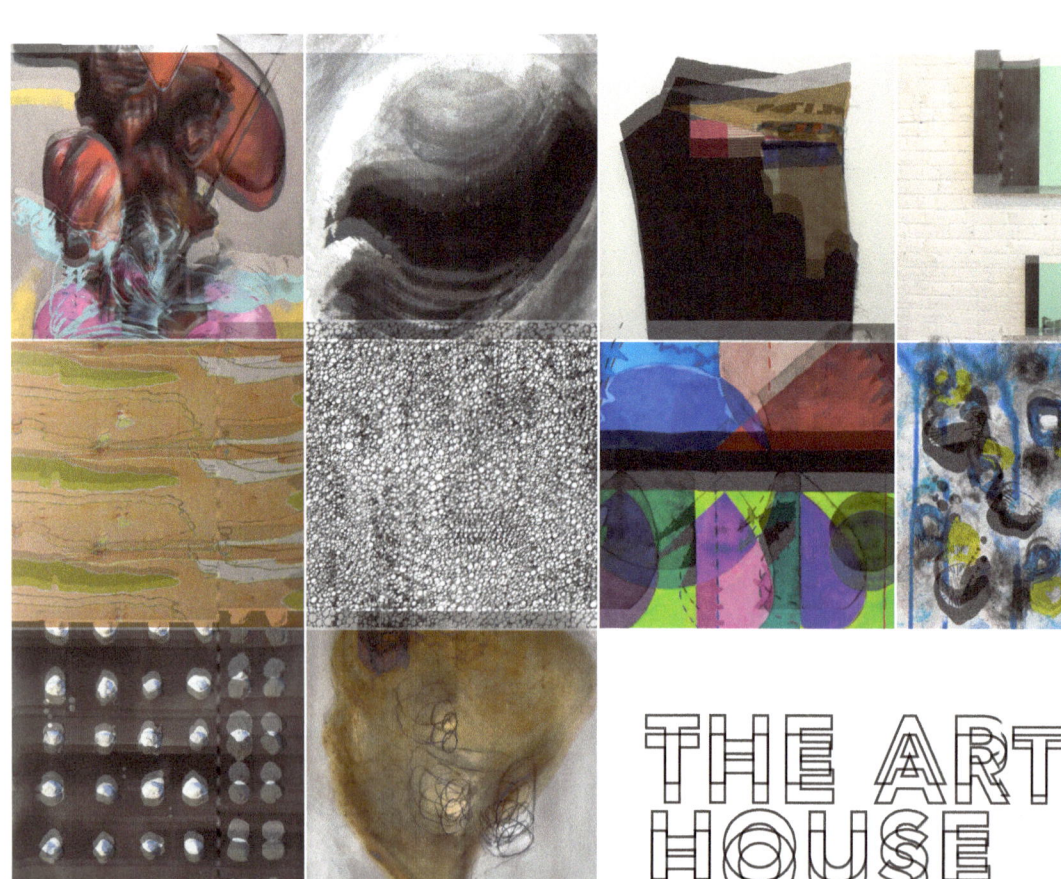

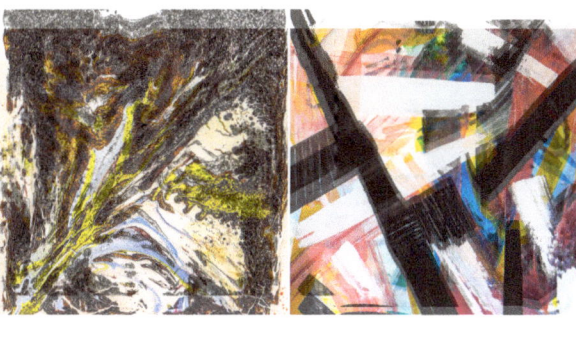

HAMILTON HOUSE

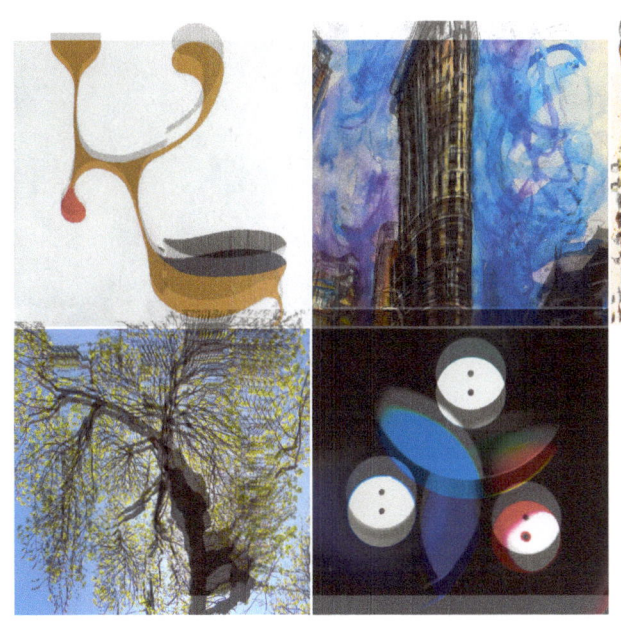

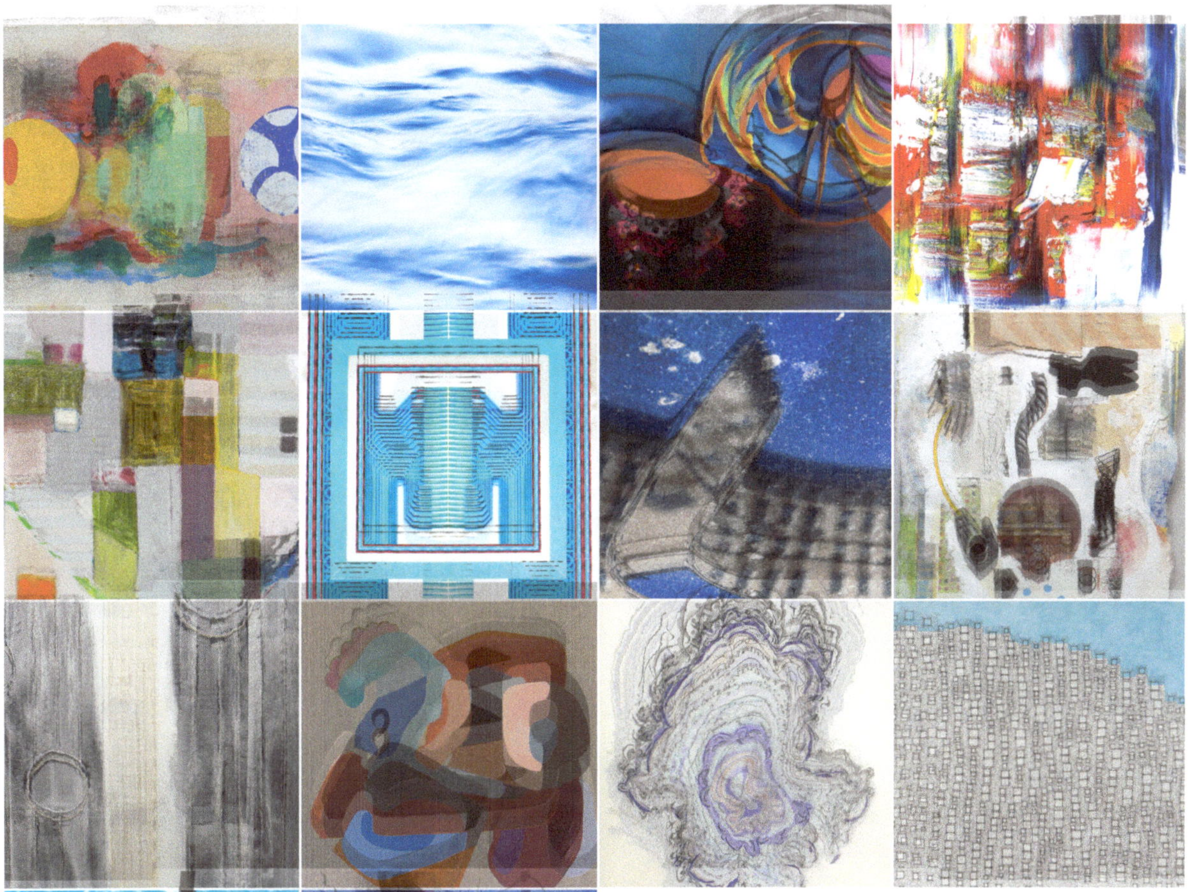

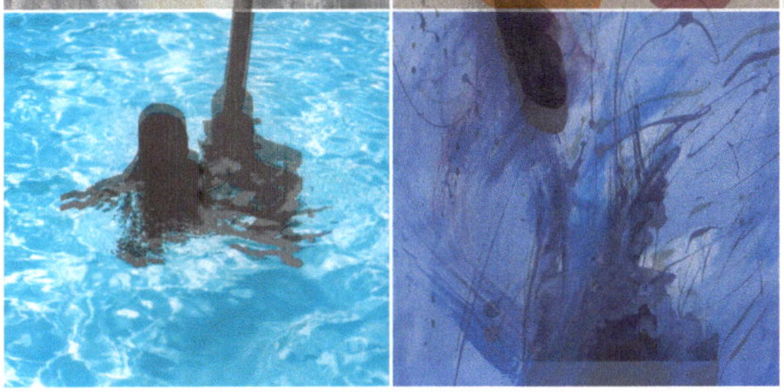

THE OAKMAN

VICTORY HALL INC. MAJOR SPONSORS AND SUPPORTERS 2017
The Geraldine R. Dodge Foundation
Qualcomm
City of Bayonne, CDBG
Hudson County LAP
Mario and Anna Scipione
Kay Cook and Perry Pogany
Alyce Gottesman

VICTORY HALL INC. STAFF
James Pustorino, Executive Director
Anne Trauben, Curator / Exhibition Director
Jill Scipione, Director, Rainbow Thursdays
Bruno Nadalin, Kimberley Wiseman,
Eileen Ferara, Maggie Ens Teaching Artists
Alejandro Rubin, Denise Yzabel Cateron, and Karen Estrada, Interns

BOARD MEMBERS
Daniel Frohwrith, President
Danielle Brooks, Vice President
John B. Starr, Jr., Ph.D, Secretary
Paul Dennison, Treasurer

COMMITTEE MEMBERS
Deirdre Kennedy
Maria Ross
Mary Hankins

Thanks to our donors for the Big Small Show and Holiday Fundraiser
Komegashi Too

Thanks to all the artists who donated artworks and to all of our 2017 yearbook sponsors!

MANY THANKS TO OUR SPONSORS

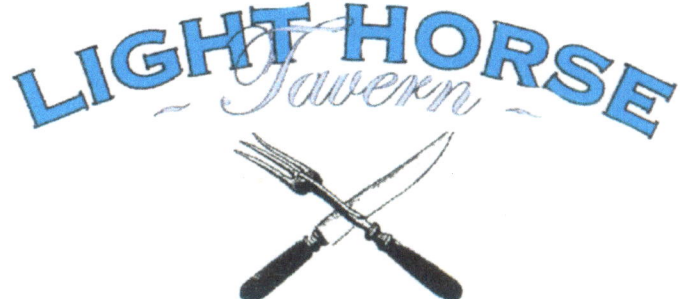

www.lighthorsetavern.com 201 946-2028
1999 Washington St. Jersey City, NJ 07302

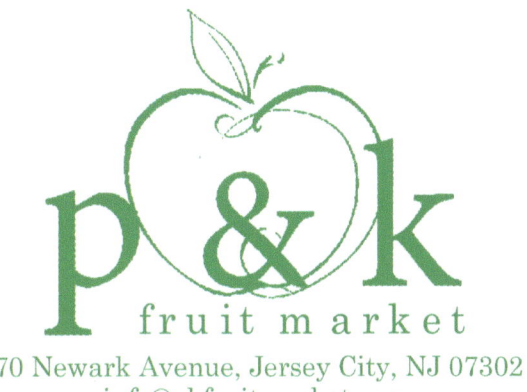

170 Newark Avenue, Jersey City, NJ 07302
info@pkfruitmarket.com

8am - 9pm daily   (201) 451-9888

eskff

EILEEN S. KAMINSKY FAMILY FOUNDATION

Is proud to support the
Victory Hall Drawing Rooms
Gallery and Programs!

Subscribe at eskff.com for news about our 2018 Fundraiser!

888 Newark Avenue Jersey City, NJ 07306 | info@eskff.com

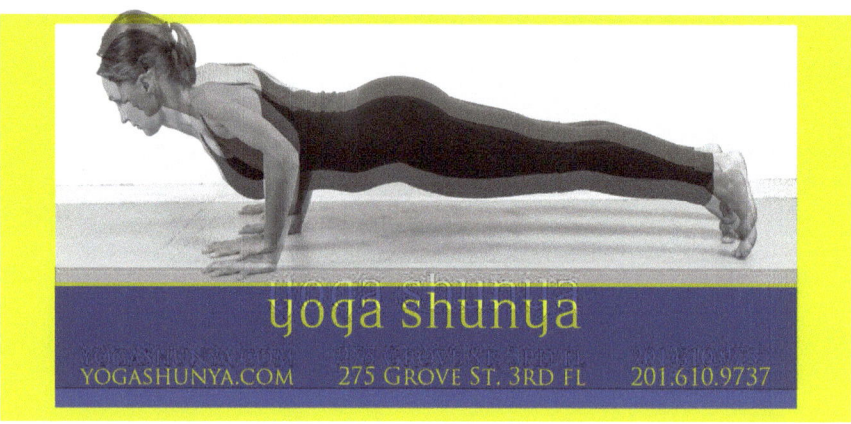

yoga shunya
YOGASHUNYA.COM 275 GROVE ST. 3RD FL 201.610.9737

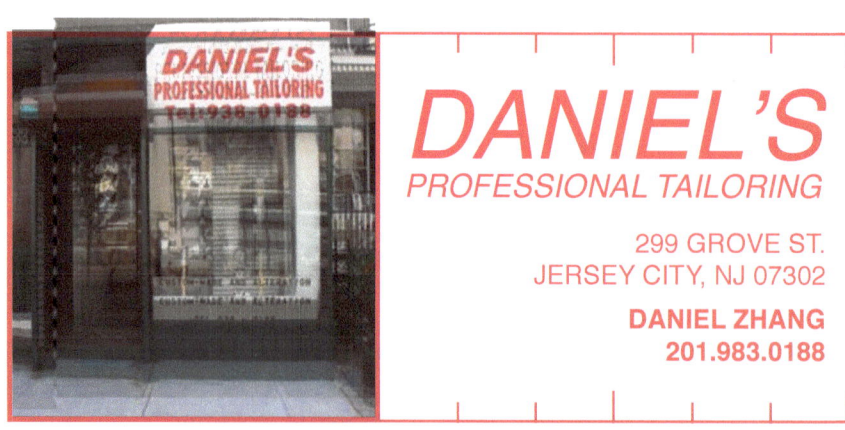

DANIEL'S
PROFESSIONAL TAILORING

299 GROVE ST.
JERSEY CITY, NJ 07302

DANIEL ZHANG
201.983.0188

BUY ART

LIVE WITH ART IN YOUR HOME. SURROUND YOURSELF WITH LIFE.

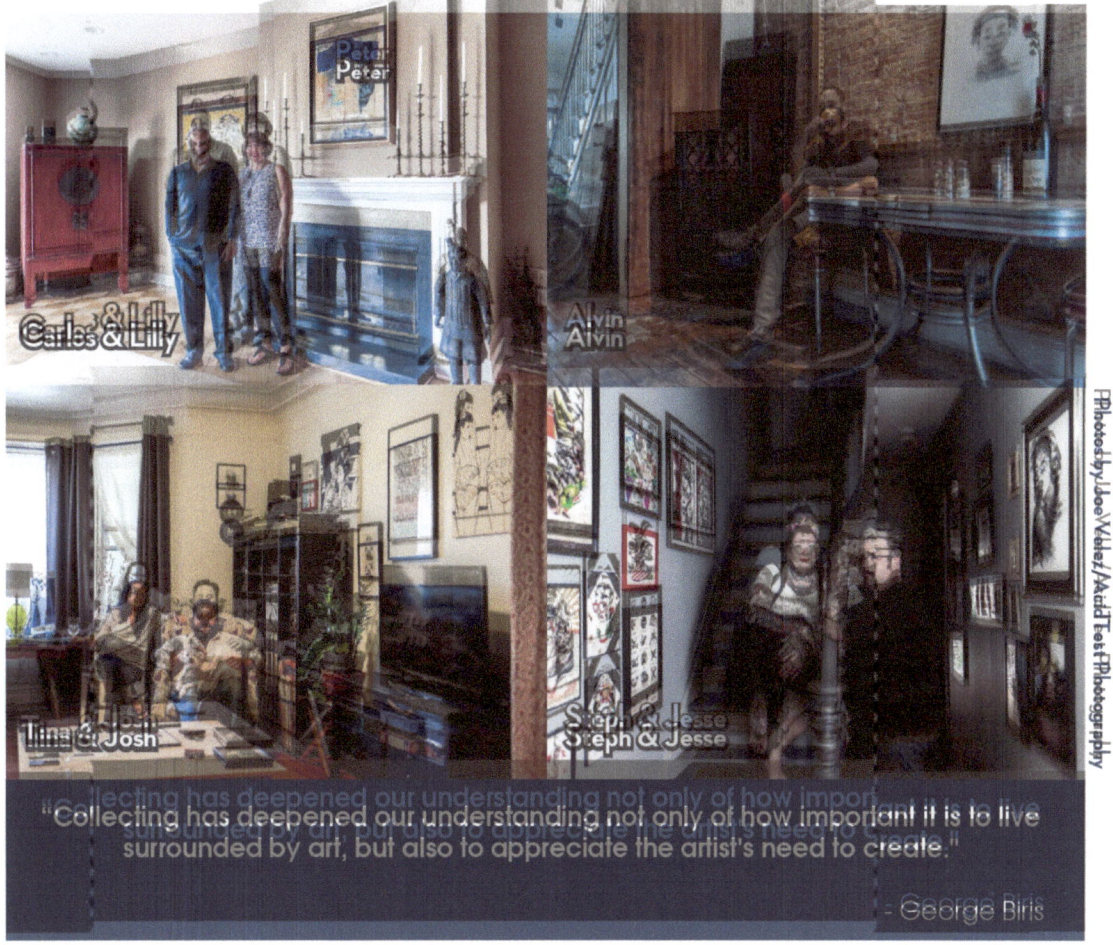

"Collecting has deepened our understanding not only of how important it is to live surrounded by art, but also to appreciate the artist's need to create."

— George Biris

Jersey City is truly the heart of art in New Jersey. The artists who live and work here are the fabric of a creative collective that makes this city vibrant, bright, dynamic, colorful and incredibly diverse. Bring this art into your personal space and you are not only supporting artists, you are contributing to a community that enriches our city with beauty. Invite the art of local artists into your home and you are bringing in their passion to tell a story.

Why value art? "You would never doubt the value of a plumber fixing the pipes in your home. For me, being surrounded by beautiful, complicated, wonderful and thought-provoking art is just as necessary as having a sink that drains."

— Jennifer Hughes

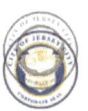 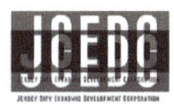 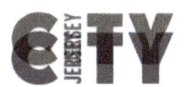

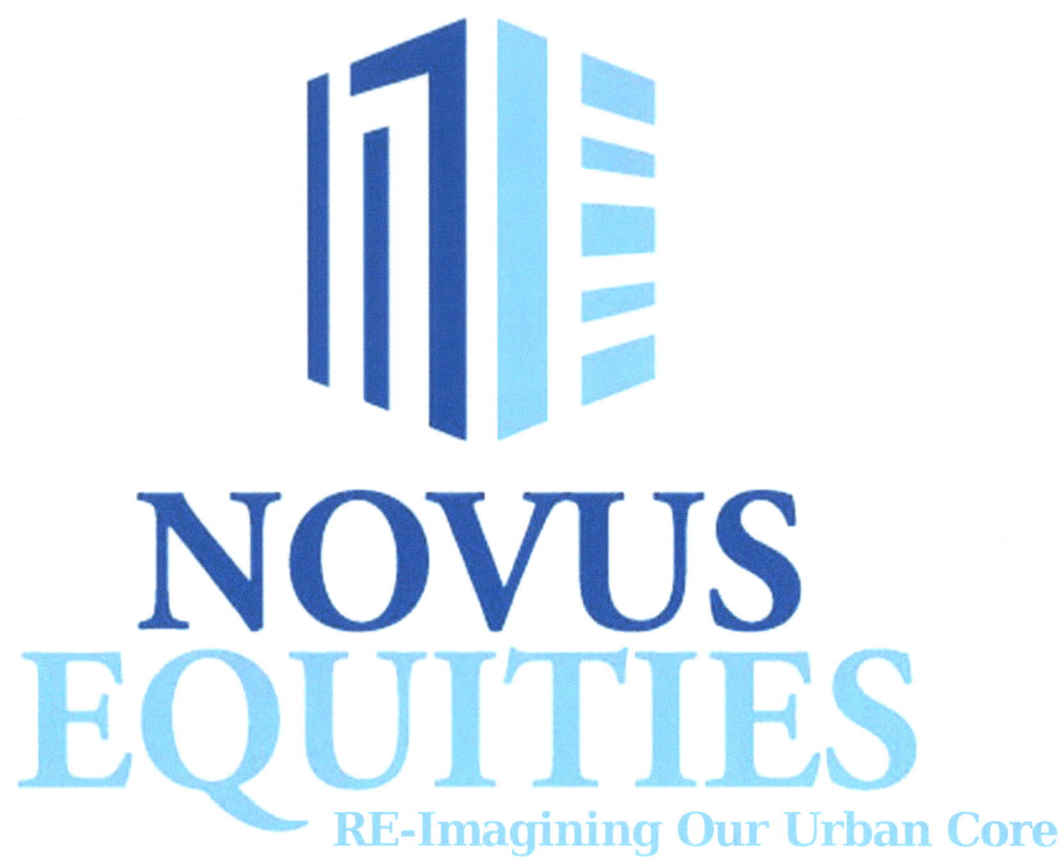

**295 Newark Avenue, Jersey City, NJ 07302
(201) 792-7700
Novusequities.com**

Novus Equities was founded on the principle of reimagining New Jersey's urban core. We at Novus are committed to providing inspired housing for the next generation by preserving the past and recycling what already exists, our own take on green living. We have rehabilitated hundreds of affordable and market rate apartments using innovative new design that reuses and repurposes all that can be saved.

Our goal -and what we do- is bringing new life to urban areas by providing commercial and residential rental properties of the highest standard, while considering the unique needs of each neighborhood we operate in.

www.ingramcontent.com/pod-product-compliance
Lightning Source LLC
Chambersburg PA
CBHW051922210526
45473CB00006B/2109